Practise Your Spelling Skills

THIRD EDITION

5

John Rose

Pearson Australia
(a division of Pearson Australia Group Pty Ltd)
707 Collins Street, Melbourne, Victoria 3008
PO Box 23360, Melbourne, Victoria 8012
www.pearson.com.au

First published 2006 by Pearson Australia
Reprinted 2007 (twice), 2008, 2009, 2010, 2011 (twice), 2013, 2014

Edited by Elizabeth Anglin
Cover and interior design by Kim Ferguson
Illustrations by Janine Dawson
Cover image by Getty Images
Prepress work by The Type Factory
Produced by Pearson Australia
Printed in Australia by the SOS Print - Media Group

ISBN 978-0-7339-7821-0

Pearson Australia Group Pty Ltd ABN 40 004 245 943

Contents

To the teacher

Spelling and writing

This spelling program, which groups words according to common visual patterns, has been prepared in response to a defined need. Spelling is one of the sub-skills of writing, along with appropriate syntactical structures, punctuation, vocabulary development and handwriting. Writing activities in the primary school should, wherever possible, emphasise the interrelatedness of these sub-skills as well as the interrelatedness of the other areas of language—listening, speaking and reading.

For written communication children need to have the desire and ability to express themselves through writing their ideas, thoughts, feelings and knowledge with increasing confidence and skill.

Spelling ability grows most effectively when spelling is viewed as an integral part of the total language program, and is developed through a continuous program that recognises both increasing ability and changing interests of the writer.

As children develop the desire to communicate their ideas in writing, they need skills in spelling that can be provided systematically. The skills and the appropriate experiences can, in many instances, go hand in hand.

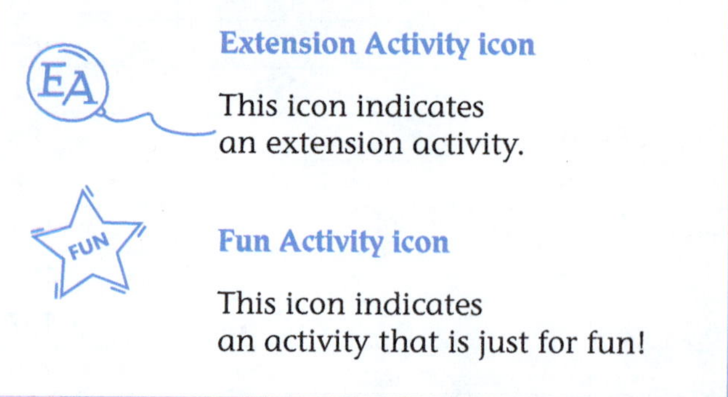

In this book ...

This book contains 36 units, four of which are revision units. Most of the remaining 32 main units begin with a list of words that contain a common visual element. Several activities in the unit are related specifically to these list words to ensure children have plenty of practice spelling the words as well as understanding word meanings and usage. There is also a variety of more general activities, including word searches, puzzles and crosswords. A number of extension activities have also been built into the units (see icon below left).

In approximately every second unit a 'Something to remember' section covers basic spelling and grammar rules, with at least two activities for the students to apply the rule in practice. In Book 5, some of the areas covered include homophones, homonyms and homographs, antonyms and synonyms, verb tenses, possessive apostrophes, compound words and numerous spelling rules.

Other units in Book 5 include an Australian History theme, the Great Barrier Reef as a theme, and two units covering commonly misspelt words and easily confused words. Challenge words are also included in a number of units to further extend fast-finishers. All of the list and challenge words are provided at the end of the book on pages 110 to 112. A helpful list of word extensions (based on the words in the book) from which many new activities could emanate is also provided on pages 113 to 115.

The units in this book are sequential in nature, covering the basic spelling requirements for students at this level. It has been designed to allow for those teachers who wish to teach spelling as a discrete subject, and for those who wish to apply the words into various writing applications.

Features of book

Word list with common letter pattern highlighted

Activities in which children explore and practise the word list words

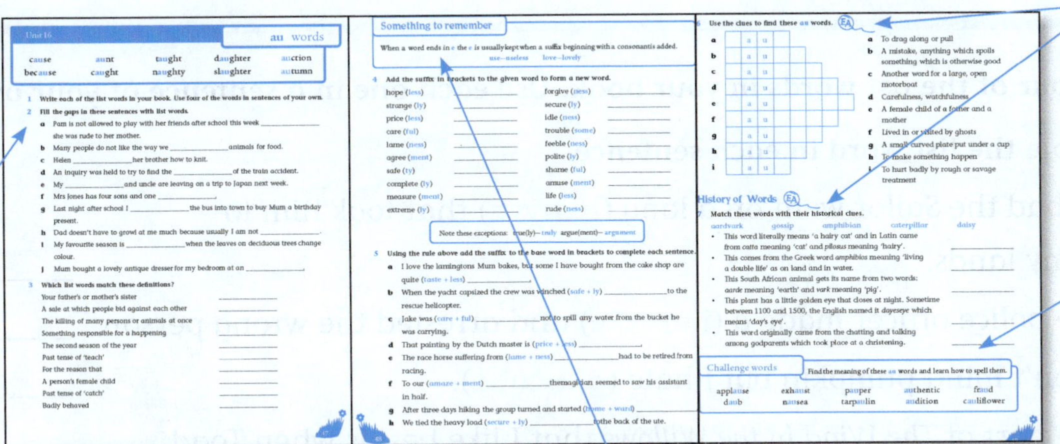

Extension activities indicated by logo

Challenge words provided throughout

'Something to remember' focuses upon another aspect of spelling

Word list for theme unit (two in book). There are also units on commonly misspelt words and easily confused words.

Further activities in which children use the list words

Activities in which children explore and practise the word list words.

Revision unit (four in book)

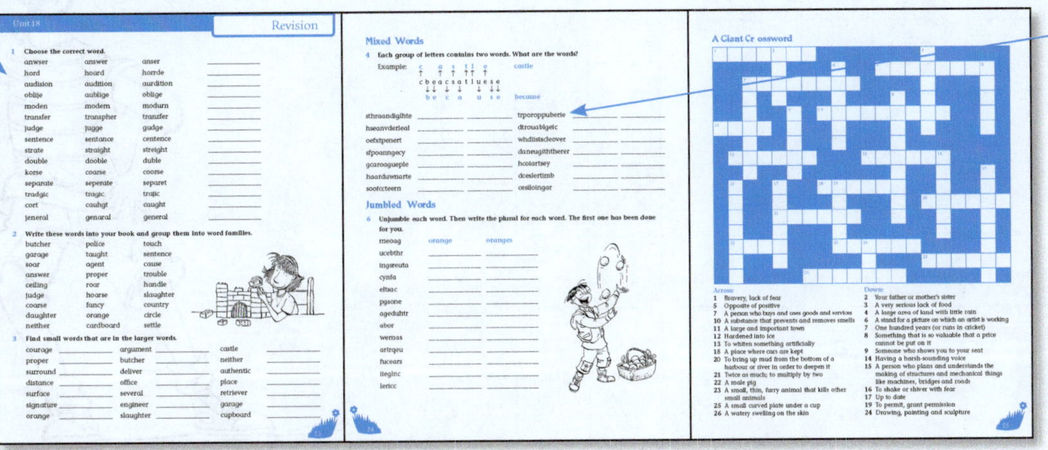

Activities in which children apply knowledge of words from earlier units

a–e words

brake	escape	surface	voyage	cabbage
mistake	scale	village	bandage	message

1 **Write four of the list words in your book. Use each one in a sentence of your own.**

2 **Unjumble the list word in each sentence.**

a Sinbad the Sailor went on a long (goavye) that took him to many lands. ______________

b The police officer made a (iamstke) and arrested the wrong person. ______________

c I don't mind pumpkin but I hate (gbbcaae). ______________

d The part of *The Wind in the Willows* that I like best is when Toad tries to (ceesap) from gaol. ______________

e The secret (msseeag) was written in code. ______________

f The cork floated on the (ecafrus) of the water. ______________

g In the small (llvigae) lived a toymaker who made a wooden puppet called Pinocchio. ______________

h To find out how far it is from Canberra to Rotorua we had to look at the (casel) on the map. ______________

3 **Complete this pattern using list words.**

				s					
				k					
				a					
				t					
				e					
				b					
				o					
				a					
				r					
				d					

4 **Can you find nine of the list words in this puzzle? Which list word has not been included?**

s	m	o	a	b	a	g	e
v	i	l	l	a	g	e	s
o	s	m	e	n	t	p	c
y	t	e	s	d	e	n	a
a	a	s	c	a	l	e	b
g	k	s	a	g	e	s	b
e	e	a	p	e	a	t	a
s	o	g	e	r	e	t	g
p	r	e	b	r	a	k	e

__________ __________

__________ __________

__________ __________

__________ __________

____

The list word not included is

__________.

5 **Use the clues to complete these list words.**

a A collection of houses and buildings in the country ___ ___ ___ ___ a ___ e

b The part of a vehicle which slows it down ___ ___ a ___ e

c A vegetable with green (sometimes purple) leaves ___ ___ ___ ___ a ___ e

d A long journey by sea ___ ___ ___ a ___ e

e The outside part of anything ___ ___ ___ ___ a ___ e

f A strip of cloth used on a wound ___ ___ ___ ___ a ___ e

g An error or a misunderstanding ___ ___ ___ ___ a ___ e

h A piece of news or information passed from one person to another ___ ___ ___ ___ a ___ e

i A small hard flake found on the skin of fish and snakes ___ ___ a ___ e

j To get free; to run away ___ ___ ___ a ___ e

Alphabetical Order

6 **Arrange the following groups of a–e words in alphabetical order.**

a mistake escape decorate scale plate

__________ __________ __________ __________ __________

b cabbage surface awake became taste

__________ __________ __________ __________ __________

7 **Change wild to tame in four moves and make to mend in four moves by changing one letter at a time to form a new word.**

w	i	l	d
t	a	m	e

m	a	k	e
m	e	n	d

An 'a' Puzzle

8 **a** The mixture of gases that we breathe

b The highest tip of something, such as the top point of a triangle

c A warning of danger; also something that wakes us up

d To have enough money to be able to buy something

e Very old; belonging to times long past

f An interview for an actor, singer or musician who is trying for a job

a	a							
b	a							
c	a							
d	a							
e	a							
f	a							

Alphabet Mixture 

Try this activity, it's a real challenge!

9 **Fill the spaces with letters from the alphabet. Use each letter only once to get nine words.**

a b c d e f g h i j k l m n o p q r s t u v w x y z

___ i ___ l ___ ___ e a ___ r ___ ___ la ___ e ___ a ___ il ___

___ ra ___ e b ___ ll ___ o ___ e ___ e ___ ec ___

e ___ er ___ i ___ e ___ uest ___ on ___ hic ___

ea words

breath	meant	wealth	health	breakfast
instead	steady	death	weather	already

1 **Write four of the list words in your book. Use each one in a sentence of your own.**

2 **Unjumble the list word in each sentence.**

a Mum always says, 'If you go out without your shoes on you'll catch your (edath) of cold'. ______________

b Just let me get my (hrabet) back before we start running again. ______________

c For (rakabefts) I had two slices of toast with marmalade. ______________

d I hope the (ahweter) improves for the weekend because I'm going camping. ______________

e It's too wet to walk to school today so we'll go by car (daetsni). ______________

f Fletcher wanted me to go to the movies with him but I had (reaaldy) seen the film. ______________

g It wasn't an accident because he (tamen) to do it. ______________

h The pensioner was in poor (alhhet) because he was not eating proper meals. ______________

i The woman had so much (wlheat) that she owned her own private aeroplane. ______________

j After the accident Kerry was not very (dtseay) on her feet. ______________

Alphabetical Order

3 **Arrange the following groups of ea words in alphabetical order.**

a	death	steady	instead	health	meant
	______	______	______	______	______
b	dream	beast	breakfast	already	deal
	______	______	______	______	______
c	gleam	dream	cream	steam	scream
	______	______	______	______	______
d	wealth	weather	weave	weak	wear
	______	______	______	______	______

Homophones

Something to remember

Homophones are words that sound the same but have different meanings and are spelt differently.

For example: **ceiling sealing** **road rode** **scent sent cent**

'Homophone' comes from two Greek words, ***homos*** meaning 'the same' and ***phone*** meaning 'sound'—words that have the same sound.

4 Circle the correct word in these sentences.

- **a** The Native Americans of North America once hunted bison and (deer, dear).
- **b** Oh (deer, dear)! I've just locked the door and my (keys, quays) are still inside.
- **c** The gusty wind was quite (chilly, chili) even though it was a sunny day.
- **d** My mum makes the best curry by adding green (chilly, chili) to the recipe.
- **e** Danni not only eats the orange, but she eats the (peal, peel) as well.
- **f** In the distance I could (hear, here) the (peal, peel) of the church bells.
- **g** When the clothes dryer broke I had to (wring, ring) out the wet clothes by hand.
- **h** (For, Four) her wedding anniversary Mum was given a beautiful sparkling (wring, ring).
- **i** A crane was needed to lift the heavy (steal, steel) girder into place.
- **j** The violent youths tried to (steal, steel) the man's wallet and mobile phone.

5 Use these words in sentences of your own to show the differences in meaning.

write ______________________________

right ______________________________

night ______________________________

knight ______________________________

site ______________________________

sight ______________________________

6 Rearrange the letters to find new words.

- **a** Add t to pale and get a round flat dish for food. ________________
- **b** Add t to nose and get a small piece of rock. ________________
- **c** Add t to rage and get a word meaning much more than usual. ________________
- **d** Add t to seal and get a word meaning not fresh. ________________
- **e** Add t to foal and get a word meaning to stay on the surface of a liquid. ________________

f Add t to **bale** and get a piece of furniture on legs with a flat top. ________________

g Add t to **wear** and get a transparent liquid without taste or smell. ________________

7 **Can you find all of the list words in this puzzle? What other ea words can you find? Colour the words you find.**

d	o	r	e	w	e	a	r	i	c	e	p
r	e	b	a	e	a	t	s	n	r	a	l
e	b	r	e	a	k	f	a	s	t	s	o
a	h	e	a	l	t	h	s	t	a	y	u
m	e	a	n	t	e	s	t	e	a	d	y
s	l	t	o	h	a	d	e	a	t	h	g
o	i	h	a	l	r	e	a	d	y	s	h
w	e	a	t	h	e	r	s	t	e	a	m

Anagrams

An anagram is what you get when you change the order of the letters in a word to make a new word. For example: **meat—tame**

8 **a** Change **lamps** into tropical trees. ________________

b Change **mile** into a citrus fruit. ________________

c Change **left** into a kind of cloth. ________________

d Change **recall** into an underground room where wine is kept. ________________

e Change **leaf** into a small biting insect. ________________

Word Quiz

EA

9 **How quickly can you find these words?**

a A five-letter word ending in *osk* ________________

b A seven-letter word ending in *rel* ________________

c A five-letter word ending in *owd* ________________

d A five-letter word ending in *uad* ________________

e A seven-letter word ending in *som* ________________

f A five-letter word ending in *ork* ________________

g A five-letter word ending in *oan* ________________

h A five-letter word ending in *dth* ________________

o–e words

wrote	telephone	whole	glove	explode
spoke	stroke	choke	throne	doze

1 Write four of the list words in your book. Use each one in a sentence of your own.

Definitions

2 Circle the correct definition to go with the list word.

a A telephone is:

- a short message which you give to the post office to send by telegraph
- an instrument that brings pictures through the air
- an instrument that carries your voice through electric wires
- an instrument you look through to see the stars.

b Whole means:

- something dug in the ground
- the largest animal in the ocean
- a part of something
- all of something; not divided.

c A glove is:

- a covering for the hand
- a round object like a ball
- something you wear on your head
- a type of flower with five petals.

d Explode means:

- to look at closely and carefully
- to give the meaning of something
- to blow up with a large bang
- costing a lot of money.

e Stroke means:

- to walk slowly
- to hit hard, usually with your fists
- to rub gently
- to hit someone with your foot.

f **Choke** means:

- to find it hard to breathe because there is something in your throat
- to cut something with hard blows
- to laugh quietly to yourself
- to get down on your knees.

g A **throne** is:

- to throw something away
- a sharp woody prickle on a plant
- a special chair for a queen or king
- a long bench at a railway station.

Jumbled Letters

3 **Use the letters in this box to make five list words. One letter is left over. In your book write ten words that begin with the extra letter.**

eeeeeee	b	w
ooooo	g	c
v	tt	r
lll	p	k
nn	hhhh	

_______________ _______________ _______________

_______________ _______________

Can You Do This One?

4 **All of these o–e words end in one. Can you find them?**

a A part of a skeleton ___ one

b A small piece of rock ___ ___ one

c Something a king or queen sits on ___ ___ ___ one

d A large area of the world ___ one

e Lying stretched out, face downwards ___ one

f All by yourself; with nobody else ___ ___ one

g A short way of writing telephone ___ ___ one

h A sound, usually musical ___ one

i Something round at the bottom and pointed at the top ___ one

j A low humming sound ___ ___ one

5 **Fill the gaps with words from the list.**

- **a** Ben thought he was going to ________________ when he swallowed the fish bone.
- **b** The police officer ________________ in a soft, gentle voice to the lost child at the show.
- **c** Yesterday I ________________ an email to my friend in Canada.
- **d** After dinner I could only eat half an apple but Carla ate a ________________ one.
- **e** The wicketkeeper took off his ________________ before he threw the ball back to the bowler.
- **f** Dad was so tired last night that he started to ________________ while watching his favourite TV show.
- **g** My cat likes me to ________________ her fur.
- **h** Shannon ran to answer the ________________ when it started to ring.
- **i** Everyone stood until the queen was seated on her ________________.
- **j** We could hear the bomb ________________ more than a kilometre away.

Glido Words

6 **Use the clues to find the missing words.**

- **a** A room just under the roof of a house
- **b** Action that makes something happen
- **c** The shore of a sea
- **d** A book of maps
- **e** A powder used to make chocolate
- **f** A food made from flour
- **g** Green covering of lawns and fields
- **h** A metal fastening for a door
- **i** Not together; in pieces

a	a				
b		a			
c			a		
d				a	
e					a
f				a	
g			a		
h		a			
i	a				

u–e words

use	useful	refuse	excuse	future
injure	picture	confuse	reduce	creature

1 **Write four of the list words in your book. Use each one in a sentence of your own.**

2 **Unjumble the list word in each sentence.**

a A bunyip is a strange (ruarcete) that is supposed to live in Australian swamps. ______________

b The soldiers set off the explosives to try to (esocnfu) the enemy. ______________

c What (sue) does this tool have? ______________

d We know what is happening now but the (uuftre) is unknown to us. ______________

e Colin McCahon, a famous New Zealand artist, painted the (icptrue) *One*. ______________

f Wayne was careful not to (niujre) himself while moving the heavy boxes. ______________

g Marie has been late for school three times this week without having a good (eescxu). ______________

h A bottle opener is a very (lusuef) thing to take with you on a picnic. ______________

i The driver had to (udrece) speed as she approached the sharp corner. ______________

j 'I (reeufs) to pay the fine', the angry man told the judge. ______________

Hidden Words

3 **Which six list words are hidden here? Each word is in two parts.**

ex	con	ture
jure	cuse	re
fu	ful	duce
use	fuse	in

______________ ______________ ______________

______________ ______________ ______________

Homonyms

Something to remember

Homonyms are words that have the same sound and the same spelling, but different meanings.

For example: batter—meaning a person who bats in a game
When Melanie went out, Jacob was the next batter.
batter—meaning flour, egg and milk mixed together to make a paste.
Graham used two eggs when he was mixing the batter.

4 Read these sentences. Then write a definition for each of the coloured words.

a Before my aunt was elected to Parliament she spoke at a lot of meetings.

____

b A spoke broke in half when I rode my bike into a tree.

____

c The police officer felled her attacker with one stroke.

____

d The stroke left her right side paralysed.

____

e My little sister likes to stroke her doll's hair.

____

f The letter H ends with a downward stroke.

____

g The Boston Strangler would choke his victims from behind.

____

h The fisherman pulled out the choke before he started the motor.

____

5 Write sentences using each of these words.

a bay—meaning an inward curve of the seashore

____

b bay—meaning to give a long, low bark

____

c tick—meaning the sound of a clock

____

d tick—meaning a small mark made when checking a list

____

e web—meaning the net spun by a spider

____

f web—meaning the skin between the toes of animals such as ducks

____

g sovereign—meaning a king or a queen

____

h sovereign—meaning an old gold coin

____

i face—meaning the front of the head

____

j face—meaning to look towards something

____

Alphabetical Order

6 Arrange these u–e words in alphabetical order.

refuse excuse future confuse picture

__________ __________ __________ __________ __________

Definitions

7 Draw a line to match the list word with the correct definition.

a	creature	To say you will not do something
b	useful	To employ something for a purpose
c	picture	A drawing, painting or photograph
d	refuse	Helpful; of practical use
e	confuse	To harm or to damage
f	use	An animal of any kind
g	injure	To mistake one thing for another
h	reduce	A drawing, painting or photograph
i	excuse	To harm or to damage

Challenge words

Find the meaning of these u–e words and learn how to spell them.

immune dispute ridicule exclude tribute
acute conclude globule presume volume

y = 'e' words

early	hungry	nearly	empty	duty
study	city	angry	lonely	company

1 **Write four of the list words in your book. Use each one in a sentence of your own.**

2 **Fill the gaps with words from the list.**

a The police officer was on traffic ________________ at the intersection after the football match.

b Robinson Crusoe led a ________________ life on the island until he met Man Friday.

c This year our netball team ________________ got into the finals.

d If you go for a walk ________________ in the morning at Bandewollock, you can see the sun rising over the distant hills.

e My sister has to ________________ for a science exam tomorrow.

f Many people like the country but I prefer the hustle and bustle of ________________ life.

g When the lost bushwalkers were rescued and brought to safety they were tired and ________________.

h The magician pulled a rabbit out of the ________________ box.

i I was glad to have Kim's ________________ on the long bus trip.

j The residents of the town were ________________ when the old trees were cut down.

What Am I?

3 **Use the clues to find the list word.**

My first letter is in *place* and also in *circus*.

My second's in *rose* but not in *rise*.

My third's in *command* and also in *plumber*.

My fourth's in *point* and also in *spear*.

My fifth's in *lane* but not in *lonely*.

My sixth's in *sundae* and also in *ring*.

My seventh's in *cyclone* and also in *pastry*.

What am I? ________________

Word Additions

4 Which list words go with each of these groupings of words?

buildings + people + traffic = ________________

annoyed + furious + bad tempered = ________________

friends + group + gathering = ________________

before time + premature + too soon = ________________

starving + famished + ravenous = ________________

friendless + single + alone = ________________

bare + unoccupied + vacant = ________________

learn + research + read = ________________

5 Match the syllables to make list words.

stud	ry	________________
hung	ty	________________
near	y	________________
emp	ly	________________

6 Find the list words.

a Which two list words have an ear? ________________ ________________

b Which list word contains one? ________________

c Which list word contains pan? ________________

d Which list words begin with a vowel? ________________ ________________

____

e Which list word contains it? ________________

Add an 'o'

7 Add an o to each of these words to form a new word. The o may be added anywhere in the word, but the other letters must remain in the same order, for example, bred—bored.

hot ________________	bard ________________	but ________________
hard ________________	god ________________	shut ________________
avid ________________	carton ________________	gran ________________
mist ________________	pen ________________	son ________________

A 'b' Puzzle

8

a	b							
b	b							
c	b							
d	b							
e	b							
f	b							

a A wide inlet of a sea or lake

b A floating marker used as a warning or a guide for ships

c The hair that grows on the chin and cheeks of a man

d A slight injury to the flesh under the skin which has changed colour

e A two-wheeled vehicle driven by pedals

f An unmarried man

First Letters

9 **Place the same letters before the words in each group to form three new words.**
For example, the letter r placed before oar, are and ice will give your roar, rare and rice.

a	___ oar	___ are	___ ice
b	___ hill	___ lose	___ raft
c	___ iced	___ rain	___ well
d	___ pine	___ and	___ hare
e	___ allow	___ ear	___ ash
f	___ read	___ evil	___ raw
g	___ hip	___ light	___ lip
h	___ rind	___ rim	___ oat
i	___ rick	___ rail	___ ear
j	___ raid	___ rush	___ ride

Challenge words

In some words ending in y, the y has an 'e' sound. Find the meaning of these y words and learn how to spell them.

surgery	cemetery	authority	majority	annually
oddity	machinery	equally	ability	finally

ai words

remain	mountain	fountain	tailor	against
explain	curtain	certain	frail	strain

1 **Write four of the list words in your book. Use each one in a sentence of your own.**

2 **Use the clues to completethe each word.**

a A person who makes clothes such as suits, trousers and skirts ___ ai ___ ___ ___

b Weak, very easily broken ___ ___ ai ___

c A very high hill ___ ___ ___ ___ ___ ai ___

d A hanging piece of cloth at a window or at the front of a stage ___ ___ ___ ___ ai ___

e Sure, without any doubt ___ ___ ___ ___ ai ___

f To stay in the same place, or to be left behind ___ ___ ___ ai ___

g To stretch or pull as tightly as possible ___ ___ ___ ai ___

h In the opposite direction to, or on the opposite side to ___ ___ ai ___ ___ ___

i Water spouting up into the air continuously from one or more jets ___ ___ ___ ___ ___ ai ___

j To make clear or easy to understand ___ ___ ___ ___ ai ___

3 **What list words when put in the spaces make three-letter words reading across?**

s		g
a		e
r		n
p		t
a		d
a		k
a		e

i		e
b		t
a		e
a		e
s		p
f		x
a		t

a		e
p		t
o		e
s		y
b		n
r		b
a		t

u		e
a		e
a		k
o		t
s		n
a		d

s		y
c		t
p		t
i		l
c		t
a		t

o		f
a		t
y		k
f		n
a		l

________________ ________________ ________________

________________ ________________ ________________

Homographs

Something to remember

Homographs are words that have the same spelling but different sounds and different meanings.

For example: tear—I will tear the paper carefully.

tear—A tear ran down Selina's cheek.

4 Write sentences using each of these words.

wound—meaning the past tense of 'wind'

____

wound—meaning a gash in the flesh

____

sow—meaning to scatter seeds

____

sow—meaning a female pig

____

bass—meaning a low-sounding voice

____

bass—meaning a fish

____

refuse—meaning rubbish

____

refuse—meaning to say no, to reject

____

5 Use a dictionary to help you find two different meanings for each of these homographs.

object 1 ______________________________

2 ______________________________

minute 1 ______________________________

2 ______________________________

lead 1 ______________________________

2 ______________________________

6 **Fill the gaps with words from the list.**

a At the end of the show the actors took a bow and then the ________________ came down.

b Next week my tennis match is ________________ Ali, who is a good player.

c When Carlie couldn't do her homework, her father tried to ________________ it to her.

d People who go ________________ climbing need special equipment.

e Dad's trousers were too long in the legs so he took them to a ________________ to have them taken up.

f During the storm there was an enormous ________________ on the cables attached to the radio tower.

g The old woman's ________________ hands could hardly hold the cup.

h Many city squares have an attractive ________________.

i Even though he won a lot of money, the man decided to ________________ at work.

j I am ________________ that Stephanie's birthday is next week.

7 **Use the clues to find these ai words.**

a		a	i					
b		a	i					
c		a	i					
d		a	i					
e		a	i					
f		a	i					
g		a	i					
h		a	i					
i		a	i					

a A quick surprise attack

b To put colour on; to make a picture with colours

c A person who makes clothes

d Not succeeding; also growing weaker (e.g. eyesight)

e Loyal; keeping your promises

f A brilliantly coloured arch which sometimes appears in the sky

g Small and delicate

h A very good and holy person

i Having a very good opinion of yourself

qu words

quiet	quite	queen	quarter
quick	queue	equal	liquid

1 **Write four of the list words in your book. Use each one in a sentence of your own.**

Definitions

2 **Circle the correct definition to go with the list word.**

a Quiet means:
- with little noise
- a small bird, like a partridge
- an unpleasant nervous feeling
- a quarter of a circle.

b A queen is:
- a container for arrows
- a strange dream
- a female ruler of a country
- a person born in Queenstown.

c A quarter is:
- a figure with four sides
- a fourth part of a whole
- a ten cent coin
- a creature being hunted.

d A queue is:
- the seventeenth letter of the alphabet
- a place where boats can load and unload
- a small type of cucumber
- a line of waiting people.

e Equal means:
- to rub out
- an imaginary line around the centre of the earth
- the same in number
- a small type of sailing boat.

f Liquid is:
- an alcoholic drink
- something flowing with no fixed shape
- a soft black lolly
- something hard and wet like ice.

3 **Write all of the list words in alphabetical order.**

______________ ______________ ______________ ______________

______________ ______________ ______________ ______________

4 **Fill in the blanks with the list words that match these definitions.**

A line of people waiting ______________

One of four equal parts ______________

Something that flows, like water ______________

Without noise ______________

A female ruler or a king's wife ______________

Fast, rapid or lively ______________

The same in size, number or value ______________

Completely or entirely ______________

Word Steps

5 **Use the clues to find these qu words. A dictionary would also be useful.**

a	q	u						
b	q	u						
c	q	u						
d	q	u						
e	q	u						
f	q	u						
g	q	u						
h	q	u						
i	q	u						

a A short test of knowledge; a set of questions to be answered

b A small wild bird of the partridge family

c To tremble or shake

d To prove yourself, for example, to win enough sporting matches during the season to be able to play in the finals

e To inquire; something you ask

f An angry dispute or argument

g A case for arrows

h The sound made by a duck

i A landing place for ships to load and unload

Word Chain

6 **Change lick to task in five moves by changing one letter at a time.**

l	i	c	k
t	a	s	k

Change a Letter

7 **a** Change one letter in *dot* to get a female deer. **dot** ______________

b Change one letter in *try* to get a word meaning to raise with a lever. **try** ______________

c Change one letter in *foe* to get a word meaning low, wet clouds. **foe** ______________

d Change one letter in *fare* to get a word meaning to grow dimmer. **fare** ______________

e Change one letter in *mine* to get a place where money is made. **mine** ______________

f Change one letter in *dream* to get the rich part of milk. **dream** ______________

g Change one letter in *eight* to get a word meaning not dark. **eight** ______________

h Change one letter in *grain* to get a part of the body. **grain** ______________

Challenge words

Find the meaning of these **qu** words and learn how to spell them.

squall	quartz	bouquet	quaint	quarantine
quarry	mosquito	query	mosque	enquire

Australian history

discovery	colony	Aborigine	explore	rebellion
convict	governor	settlement	marine	grazier

1 **Write four of the list words in your book. Use each one in a sentence of your own.**

2 **What list words match these definitions?**

To search for something ________________

Newly settled part of a country ________________

A settlement of people in a new land ________________

Finding out; something found ________________

Farmer who raises cattle for the market ________________

A soldier on a warship ________________

A condemned criminal ________________

One of the first or earliest inhabitants of a country ________________

A person who governs or rules ________________

A revolt or fight against the people who rule ________________

3 **Write the list words in alphabetical order.**

________________ ________________ ________________ ________________ ________________

________________ ________________ ________________ ________________ ________________

How Many Syllables?

4 **Next to each list word, write how many syllables you sound in that word.**

explore		convict		grazier	
discovery		colony		rebellion	
aborigine		settlement		marine	

Doubling Final Consonants

Something to remember

After a short vowel, the last consonant is doubled when adding ed or ing.

chop chopped chopping

5 **Complete this list.**

chop	chopped	chopping
permit	______________	______________
regret	______________	______________
strip	______________	______________
skip	______________	______________
pin	______________	______________
occur	______________	______________
admit	______________	______________
commit	______________	______________
prefer	______________	______________

6 **Using the rule above, extend the words in brackets in these sentences.**

a Tomorrow Jessica is going (swim) ________________ at the pool.

b We could see the wallaby (hop) ________________ across the sandy plain.

c When we were walking through the forest we (spot) ________________ a lyrebird building a ground nest.

d Ricky Ponting (bat) ________________ for four hours to make his century.

e The happy girl was (skip) ________________ along the street.

f The car was (travel) ________________ at a very fast speed when the tyre burst.

g When Chloe (drop) ________________ the vase it shattered.

h Claire didn't have any breakfast because she was (run) ________________ late for school.

A 'c' Puzzle

7 **a** A male swan; also the inner part of an ear of corn

b A very small room in a prison or a monastery

c To cut meat into slices

d A small church or a separate part of a large church

e Mounted soldiers

f To fall or break down; a failure

a	c							
b	c							
c	c							
d	c							
e	c							
f	c							

Build a Word

8 **You might need to rearrange some letters.**

Write down a word meaning a male child.

Add a letter to get a part of the face.

Add a letter to get a rope used to hang a person.

Tri and Try 

9 **Each word begins with tri or ends with try. Use the clues to find what they are.**

a A tri with three legs tri ______________

b A try with two legs who guards ______________ try

c A tri that is sweet to eat tri ______________

d A try that is baked to eat ______________ try

e A tri that is a weapon tri ______________

f A try where food is kept ______________ try

g A tri meaning crafty or difficult tri ______________

h A try that means cold and stormy ______________ try

i A tri that is a group of people tri ______________

j A try that is very hot and close weather ______________ try

Revision

1 Choose the correct word.

explayne	explain	explane	________
meant	ment	meent	________
already	allready	alredie	________
qiet	quiete	quiet	________
tailor	tailer	taler	________
creeture	kreature	creature	________
pickture	picture	pictore	________
wrote	rote	wroate	________
doze	doose	dooze	________
marine	merine	murine	________
cabage	cabbige	cabbage	________
bandade	bandage	bandidge	________
use	youse	uese	________
lonly	lonely	lonelly	________
citie	sity	city	________

2 Write these words into your book and group them into word families.

wrote	mistake	telephone
hungry	mountain	frail
quarter	company	quick
picture	voyage	brake
refuse	weather	liquid
glove	choke	curtain
future	angry	breath
escape	breakfast	confuse

3 Find small words that are in the larger words.

brake	________	escape	________	reduce	________
wrote	________	scale	________	glove	________
mistake	________	village	________	message	________
whole	________	spoke	________	quite	________
useful	________	bandage	________	throne	________
surface	________	refuse	________	creature	________
nearly	________	strain	________	quarter	________
weather	________	explain	________	lonely	________

Mixed Words

4 Each group of letters contains two words. What are the words?

Example:

```
 b     r a       k   e      brake
 ↑     ↑ ↑       ↑   ↑
 b e x r a p l o k d e e
   ↓ ↓     ↓ ↓ ↓   ↓   ↓
   e x     p l o   d   e    explode
```

vciolulpaglee	____________	____________	doliubqluied	____________	____________
tarielodruce	____________	____________	stmreoksseage	____________	____________
kpictunifree	____________	____________	crheautunregry	____________	____________
faogunatAininst	____________	____________	qbreauekfueast	____________	____________
cmouirsagtaeke	____________	____________	cdiabbviagdee	____________	____________
tueselfephuonle	____________	____________	emagaptinyst	____________	____________

Jumbled Words

5 Unjumble each word. Then write the plural for each word. The first one has been done for you.

nanomuti	mountain	mountains
ueeqn	____________	____________
rlitao	____________	____________
linbeerio	____________	____________
niatcur	____________	____________
icty	____________	____________
ntvcioc	____________	____________
xuecse	____________	____________
reeruact	____________	____________
vogle	____________	____________
zreragi	____________	____________
ypocman	____________	____________
vyoega	____________	____________

A Giant Word Search

6 **How many words can you find in this giant word search? The words go across the page or down the page. Colour in the words as you find them.**

E	X	C	U	S	E	N	O	T	Q	H	I
A	F	O	B	R	A	K	E	Q	U	A	L
M	O	U	N	T	A	I	N	C	I	T	Y
S	U	R	R	O	U	N	D	U	T	Y	U
U	N	A	S	U	R	F	A	C	E	N	S
S	T	G	G	E	X	E	R	C	I	S	E
E	A	E	P	I	N	S	T	E	A	D	F
D	I	V	I	D	E	S	C	A	L	E	U
O	N	O	C	E	X	P	L	O	D	E	L
Z	S	Y	T	A	C	L	T	O	U	C	H
E	T	A	U	T	I	N	J	U	R	E	O
F	U	G	R	H	T	A	I	L	O	R	V
T	D	E	E	R	E	A	R	L	Y	T	E
E	Y	O	Q	J	A	N	G	E	O	A	C
L	I	Q	U	I	D	T	U	S	U	I	R
E	Q	U	E	U	E	T	I	C	N	N	E
P	B	I	E	E	N	R	D	A	G	F	A
H	E	E	N	D	N	I	E	P	I	R	T
O	L	T	R	O	U	B	L	E	S	A	U
N	B	L	Q	U	S	E	A	M	P	I	R
E	R	A	C	B	I	T	W	H	O	L	E
N	E	I	G	L	O	V	E	O	K	O	N
Q	A	R	M	E	S	S	A	G	E	N	E
U	T	W	E	A	L	W	R	I	T	E	T
A	H	E	A	E	O	N	E	A	R	L	Y
R	M	A	N	S	P	G	M	V	Z	Y	C
T	I	L	T	S	T	R	A	I	N	E	O
E	S	T	C	T	I	O	I	L	E	M	U
R	T	H	A	E	R	U	N	L	V	P	N
C	A	C	B	A	E	P	N	A	E	T	T
O	K	U	B	D	Z	A	N	G	R	Y	R
U	E	R	A	Y	A	L	R	E	A	D	Y
P	E	T	G	O	C	O	N	F	U	S	E
L	P	A	E	T	H	R	O	N	E	X	T
E	U	I	B	R	E	A	K	F	A	S	T
B	A	N	D	A	G	E	K	N	I	F	E

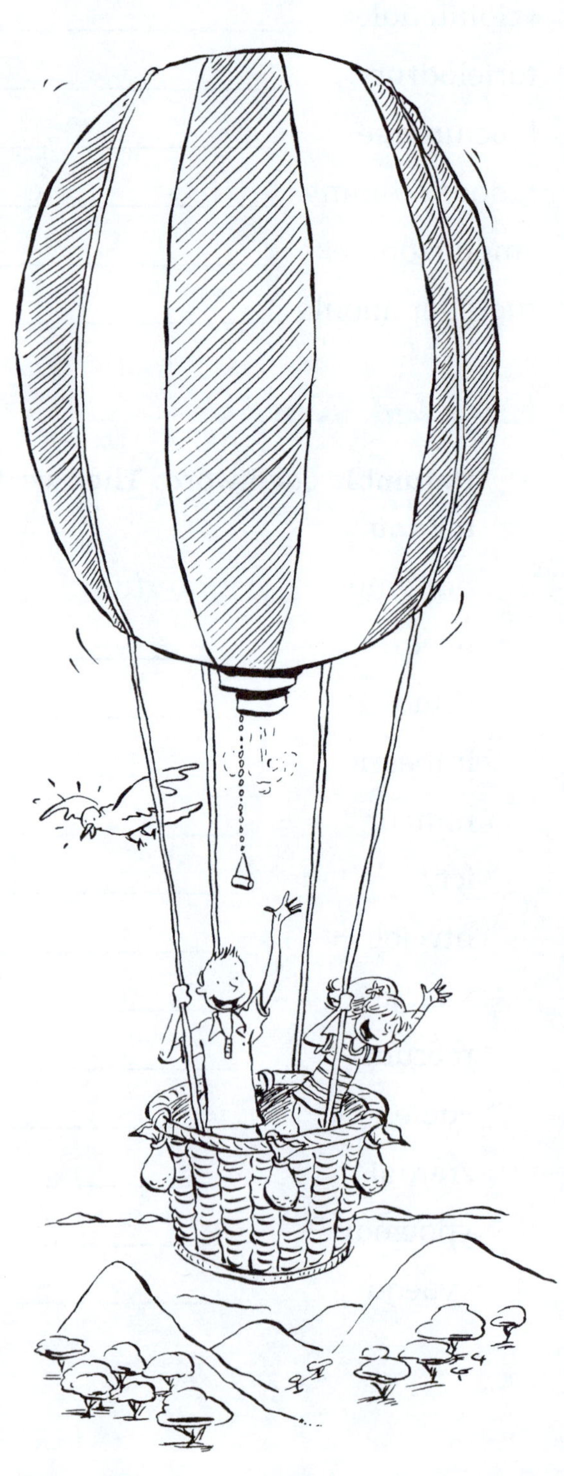

ou words

mountain	surround	country	trouble	double
touch	group	young	courage	couple

1 **Write four of the list words in your book. Use each one in a sentence of your own.**

2 **Use the clues to complete each word.**

a A nation or state with its land or population ___ ou ___ ___ ___ ___

b Bravery, lack of fear ___ ou ___ ___ ___ ___

c A very high hill ___ ou ___ ___ ___ ___ ___

d In the early part of life or growth ___ ou ___ ___

e To feel with the fingers ___ ou ___ ___

f Twice as much, to multiply by two ___ ou ___ ___ ___

g Two of a kind together, a pair ___ ou ___ ___ ___

h To be all around something ___ ___ ___ ___ ou ___ ___

i A cause of worry ___ ___ ou ___ ___ ___

j A number of persons or things together ___ ___ ou ___

What Am I?

3 **Use the clues to find the list word.**

My first letter is in *ace* but not in *age*.

My second's in *hollow* and also in *smoke*.

My third's in *usual* and also in *buoy*.

My fourth's in *tune* but not in *tube*.

My fifth's in *faint* and also in *sultry*.

My sixth's in *sheer* but not in *sheep*.

My seventh's in *skylark* and also in *verify*.

What am I? ______________

4 **Which six list words are hidden here?**

Each word is in two parts.

______________ ______________

______________ ______________

______________ ______________

trou	sur	ain
ble	coun	dou
mount	age	try
cour	round	ble

Something to remember

If a word ends in a silent e, the e is dropped before adding ing.

dine dining

5 Complete this table.

dine	dining	scrape	______
shine	______	bathe	______
hire	______	combine	______
indicate	______	feature	______
chase	______	trace	______
bale	______	barricade	______
exercise	______	decline	______
explode	______	drone	______
measure	______	reduce	______

6 Using the rule above, extend the words in brackets in these sentences.

a Courtney is (hope) ______ that it will rain tomorrow so the cross-country run will be cancelled.

b Once my (write) ______ improved, my teacher gave me a pen license.

c Christina's father is (drive) ______ us all to the shopping centre on Saturday.

d Brodie and Alana did a great job (dance) ______ in the competition.

e My little brother said he would like a job (taste) ______ all the lollies at Willy Wonka's Chocolate Factory.

f Nathan was (use) ______ a power saw when the electricity went off.

Word Square

7 List as many words as you can from the letters in the word square. Each word must be made up of letters in squares which touch each other.

m	e	r	a
a	t	m	p
r	e	a	s
k	s	o	t

______ ______ ______ ______

______ ______ ______ ______

______ ______ ______ ______

______ ______ ______ ______

______ ______ ______ ______

8 **What list words, when put in the spaces, make three-letter words reading across?**

i		e
p		d
c		t
a		t
a		e
t		y
b		e

i		e
c		w
f		r
a		e
r		n
e		g
t		n

o		d
l		g
o		t
e		b
a		e
b		d

a		e
b		w
m		g
a		e
i		l
t		n

e		e
d		t
b		s
a		d
a		e

Word Steps

9 **The end of one word begins the next word.**

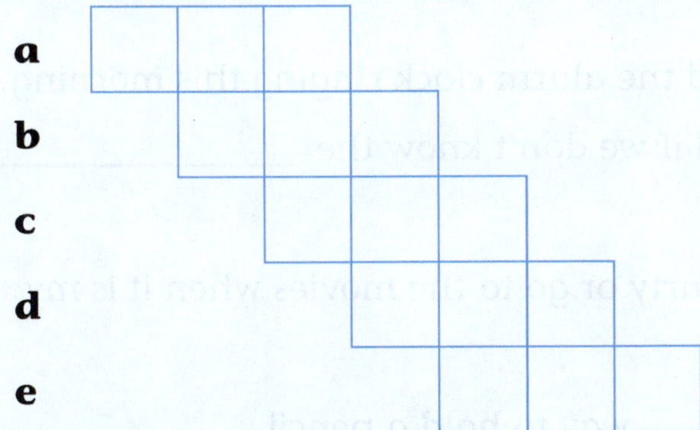

a

b

c

d

e

a A device for controlling the flow of liquid

b A large monkey without a tail

c A round green seed that grows in a pod

d A spike of grain (such as wheat)

e Drawing, painting and sculpture

Australian Towns (EA)

10 **Fit the words in List A into the correct spaces in List B to make the names of Australian towns and cities.**

List A	List B
room	Br ________________ bane
art	Melb ________________ ne
is	Adel ________________ e
win	B ________________ e
our	Fre ________________ tle
any	T ________________ sville
aid	Hob ________________
own	Gee ________________
long	Alb ________________
man	Dar ________________

er words

answer	several	herd	proper	general
either	butcher	modern	neither	desert

1 **Write four of the list words in your book. Use each one in a sentence of your own.**

2 **Complete these sentences with list words.**

- **a** Most animals that live in the hot ________________ seek their food at night.
- **b** The ________________ of cattle was grazing in the paddock near the river flats.
- **c** ________________ people went to help the elderly man after he had fallen near the bus stop.
- **d** Mum likes our ________________ because he cuts off the fat before he weighs the meat.
- **e** ________________ Ivan nor his brother heard the alarm clock ringing this morning.
- **f** Our teacher never makes us feel embarrassed if we don't know the ________________ to a question.
- **g** Dad said I could ________________ have a party or go to the movies when it is my birthday.
- **h** Andrea was never taught the ________________ way to hold a pencil.
- **i** I have a ________________ idea of how a car works.
- **j** My aunt collects ________________ art.

3 **Write five of the list words by adding the letters in Box 1 to the letters in Box 2.**

Box 1		Box 2
prop neith answ eith butch	+	er

____

____

____

____

____

Now write the remaining five list words.

______________ ______________ ______________ ______________ ______________

Definitions

4 **Circle the correct definition to go with the list word.**

a An answer is

- something you say that asks for information
- to make known publicly
- a reply to a question
- an enclosed area for shows.

b Several means

- to cut up into parts
- more than two but fewer than many
- one thing or object by itself
- not kind or gentle.

c A herd is

- a plant whose leaves are used to flavour food
- to hear what someone is saying
- an animal's skin used for leather
- a group of animals of one kind.

d Proper means

- suitable, correct
- land that is owned
- the steel blades on an aeroplane
- being able to tell the future.

e Modern means

- very old, having existed for a long time
- being shy, avoiding publicity
- to change something slightly
- of the present time, not ancient.

f A desert is

- to make very sad
- a large area of land with little rain
- the sweet dish served at a meal
- a type of large American lizard.

g General means

- an apparatus for producing electricity
- well-bred, refined in manners
- widespread, relating to the whole
- to swallow food quickly.

Glido Words

5 Use clues to complete this puzzle.

a The opposite of dark

b To permit, to grant permission

c Someone who governs

d A firm, round fruit that grows on a tree

e The outer covering of a nut or egg

f A short story that has a moral

g Wrong, untruthful

h To rest with the eyes closed

i Great in size or quantity

a	l				
b		l			
c			l		
d				l	
e					l
f				l	
g			l		
h		l			
i	l				

Occupations

6 One of the list words is butcher. A butcher is a person who cuts up meat and sells it. Complete these examples to find more occupations.

He prints.	He is a ________________.
They publish books.	They are book ________________.
She teaches.	She is a ________________.
He cleans.	He is a ________________.
She dances.	She is a ________________.
He drives.	He is a ________________.
She dives.	She is a ________________.
He plays football.	He is a ________________.
They paint.	They are ________________.
She produces TV shows.	She is a TV ________________.
He works in a mine.	He is a ________________.

Challenge words

Find the meaning of these er words and learn how to spell them.

flounder	whether	retriever	lantern	blister
premier	perhaps	consumer	diameter	transfer

soft c words

distance	city	place	police	fancy
surface	sentence	circle	office	ceiling

1 **Write each of the list words in your book. Use four list words in sentences of your own.**

Alphabetical Order

2 **Each of these words contain a soft c. Place each group of words in alphabetical order.**

a	distance	office	fancy	police	circle
	______	______	______	______	______
b	place	city	ceiling	twice	decide
	______	______	______	______	______
c	surface	sentence	silence	science	spice
	______	______	______	______	______
d	practice	piece	century	bicycle	medicine
	______	______	______	______	______
e	necessary	excite	niece	piece	justice
	______	______	______	______	______

3 **Complete these sentences using list words.**

a The ______________ of the desks were painted during the holidays.

b We left our car on the outskirts of town and walked the short ______________ to the shopping centre.

c Extra ______________ were on duty on the day of the demonstration.

d The tablecloth was decorated with a ______________ border.

e An accountant has just opened an ______________ in our suburb.

f After Dad had painted the ______________ he had spots of white paint all over his face.

g There's a ______________ of haze around the moon tonight.

h Some people like living in the country, but I prefer the ______________.

i We had to write a ______________ that contained two adjectives.

j This is the ______________ where the storm did so much damage.

Contractions

Something to remember

When writing **contractions** (words that have been made smaller) an apostrophe is put in place of the letter or letters left out. For example: you are—you're   it is—it's

4 Draw lines to match the contractions from List A with the words from List B.

List A	List B
they're	he is
wasn't	you have
he's	she would
I'm	was not
they'll	who will
we're	they are
you've	I am
who'll	we are
she'd	they will

5 Change the words in brackets to contractions to fit into these sentences.

a Did you remember that (you are) _______________ the flag monitor this week?

b If the weather stays fine (we will) _______________ have a picnic lunch today.

c 'That (is not) _______________ very funny James', said Luke.

d (I would) _______________ prefer to learn the piano rather than the violin.

e If it gets too hot (you will) _______________ have to play in the shade.

f I (can not) _______________ work out the answer to this problem.

g If (we had) _______________ only listened carefully, this would never have happened.

h Rebekah (does not) _______________ like ice cream but she loves yoghurt.

6 Which list word goes with these groups of words?

loop	ring	sphere	_______________
town	municipality	metropolis	_______________
constable	patrol	protect	_______________
judgment	decision	ruling	_______________
outside	veneer	exterior	_______________
range	space	gap	_______________

Definitions

7 **Circle the correct definition to go with the list word.**

a A city is
- a group of houses and buildings like a town but smaller
- the land used for farming
- a large and important town
- a special chair for sitting on.

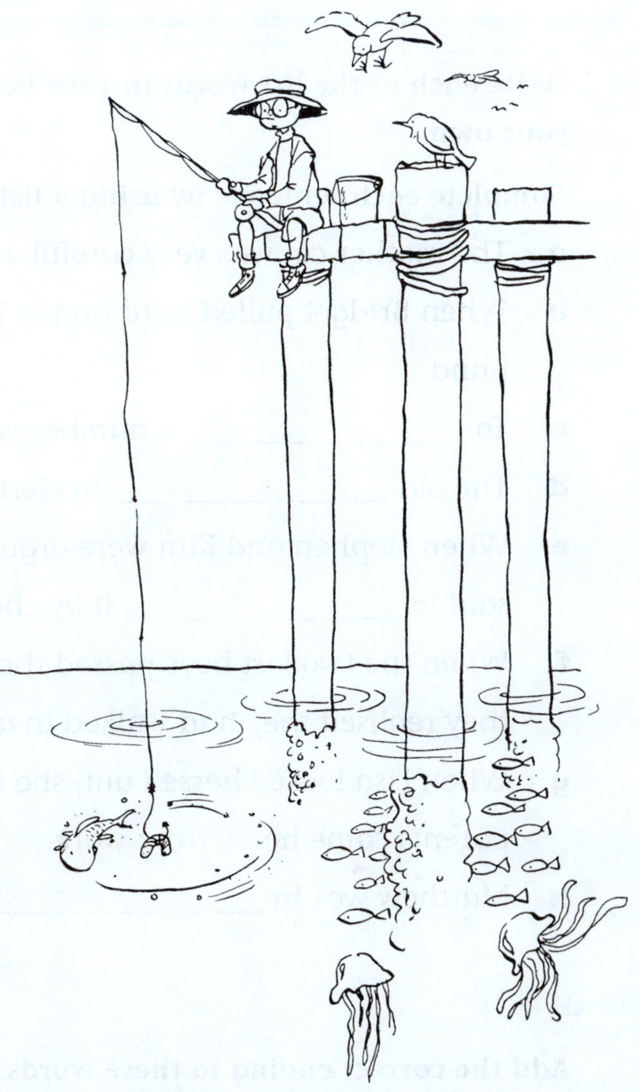

b Place means
- a particular position in space
- a particular area on a surface
- to state the position of a runner at the end of a race
- all of the above definitions.

c A circle is
- anything which is egg-shaped
- something in the shape of a ring
- a building where films are shown
- a building besides a sports field.

d Ceiling means
- to fasten or close with a seal
- to hunt for large fish-eating animals
- the surface indoors on which you stand
- the surface indoors at the top of a room.

e An office is
- a person in a position of command in the armed forces
- a place where business is done
- a person who works in government
- eggs beaten together and fried.

f A sentence is
- a punishment for a criminal found guilty of a crime
- a person who works for somebody else
- a small group of words without a verb
- a type of cloth made from flax.

le words

castle	gentle	trouble	circle
couple	double	settle	handle

1 **Write each of the list words in your book. Use four of the list words in sentences of your own.**

2 **Complete each sentence by using a list word.**

a The mother cat was very careful and ________________ with the two newborn kittens.

b When Bridget pulled hard on the jammed door, the ________________ came off in her hand.

c To ________________ a number you multiply it by two.

d The old ________________ in Germany is now the home of a wealthy businessman.

e When Stephen and Kim were arguing over how far Uluru is from Alice Springs, Mum said to ________________ it by checking in the encyclopaedia.

f When the two lost boys passed the place where they had camped for the second time, they realised they had walked in a large ________________.

g When Lisa locked herself out, she had to wait a ________________ of hours until her parents came home from work.

h Matthew was in ________________ after he dropped his library book in a puddle.

le or el?

3 **Add the correct ending to these words. If necessary use a dictionary to help you.**

bund ___ ___	cam ___ ___	cast ___
artic ___ ___	troub ___ ___	lev ___ ___
feeb ___ ___	trav ___ ___	weas ___ ___
mod ___ ___	doub ___ ___	hot ___ ___
enam ___ ___	hand ___ ___	circ ___ ___
terrib ___ ___	sentin ___ ___	mot ___ ___
need ___ ___	wrest ___ ___	rif ___ ___
funn ___ ___	wrink ___ ___	tunn ___ ___

A 'ble' Crossword

4 Use the clues to find these ble words.

a					b	l	e
b	b	l	e				
c					b	l	e
d	b	l	e				
e					b	l	e
f	b	l	e				
g				b	l	e	
h	b	l	e				
i				b	l	e	
j	b	l	e				

a To trip or take a false step

b A stain or a fault

c To disturb; to cause worry or difficulties

d To whiten something artificially

e To shake or shiver with fear

f Sore and red around the eyes

g Twice as much; to multiply by two

h Cold and unsheltered, dull and cheerless

i A ball of air or gas usually contained in a liquid shell

j To mix together, a mixture

5 Which three list words have **ou**? ________________ ________________ ________________

Which list word has a part of the body? ________________

Which list word has a double **t**? ________________

Which list word has a cast? ________________

Which list word is probably a male? ________________

Which list word contains **ir**? ________________

6 Which list words have been used to make the following words?

gentleness	gentleman	gentler	________________
handlebar	mishandled	handling	________________
couplet	coupled	coupling	________________
settlement	resettled	settler	________________
doubled	doubling	redoubled	________________
troublesome	troubled	troubling	________________
circular	circling	circled	________________

Change a Letter

7 **a** Change one letter in **puzzle** to something put on dogs to stop them biting. — **puzzle** ___ ___ ___ ___ ___ ___

b Change one letter in **barrel** to get a word meaning unable to produce vegetation. — **barrel** ___ ___ ___ ___ ___ ___

c Change one letter in **closet** to get a word meaning not open. — **closet** ___ ___ ___ ___ ___ ___

d Change one letter in **lamp** to get a sloping surface connecting two levels. — **lamp** ___ ___ ___ ___

e Change one letter in **rake** to get a word meaning great anger or fury. — **rake** ___ ___ ___ ___

f Change one letter in **hour** to get a guided visit or journey. — **hour** ___ ___ ___ ___

g Change one letter in **blind** to get a word meaning to move the eyelids quickly. — **blind** ___ ___ ___ ___ ___

h Change one letter in **number** to get a word meaning wood from the forest. — **number** ___ ___ ___ ___ ___ ___

New Zealand Towns

8 **Fit the words in List A into the correct spaces in List B to make the answers of New Zealand towns and cities.**

List A	List B
car	________________ ilton
lock	Ro ________________ rua
mouth	W ________________ arei
Ham	Inver ________________ gill
to	Ha ________________ s
burn	Have ________________
Palm	Grey ________________
it	Spring ________________
sting	Hok ________________ ika
hang	________________ erston

oar words

oar	roar	hoard	cupboard	coarse
soar	boar	board	cardboard	hoarse

1 **Write each of the list words in your book. Use four of the words in sentences of your own.**

2 **Complete these sentences with words from the list.**

a While in the mountains we watched the eagle ________________ through the sky.

b John did his project on a large sheet of white ________________.

c After Ivan had dried the dishes with Dad, they put them away in the ________________ .

d The pirates let out bloodthirsty screams as they prepared to ________________ the enemy ship.

e The wild ________________ had very sharp tusks.

f Misers like to ________________ all their money.

g Leigh was ________________ after the ice hockey match because he had been yelling too much.

h Some sandpaper is quite fine but some is very ________________.

i After the kill the lion let out a loud ________________.

j The ________________ was lost when it fell over the side of the boat.

Definitions

3 **Circle the correct definition to go with the list word.**

a An **oar** is
- a kind of tree that grows very big
- a long piece of wood with one flat end, used to row a boat
- a solemn promise that you will speak the truth
- a look of great fear and wonder.

b **Soar** means
- painful when touched
- to cut wood with a metal tool
- a red spot on your skin
- to fly high into the air.

c A **boar** is
- another word for mirror
- someone who talks about himself too much
- a male pig
- a female pig.

d **Roar** means
- not cooked
- a loud deep noise made by some animals
- standing without any clothes on
- not being able to find something.

Something to remember

When a word ends in an e, the e is usually dropped when a suffix beginning with a vowel is added.

insure—insurance   expense—expensive

4 Add the suffix in brackets to the given word to form a new word.

observe (ation)	________________	confuse (ion)	________________
value (able)	________________	vacate (ion)	________________
space (ious)	________________	move (able)	________________
ignore (ance)	________________	stole (en)	________________
dictate (ion)	________________	reside (ence)	________________
confide (ence)	________________	slave (ery)	________________
fame (ous)	________________	believe (able)	________________
decorate (ion)	________________	grace (ious)	________________
negate (ive)	________________	relate (ive)	________________
desire (able)	________________	accommodate (ion)	________________

5 Using the rule above, add the suffix to the base word in brackets to complete each sentence.

a Once the doctor gave me an injection the pain was more (endure + able) ________________.

b The lake was completely (froze + en) ________________ in the middle of winter.

c Carla's green dress was very (expense + ive) ________________ and she only wore it once.

d The doctor used a small torch to carry out her (examine + ation) ________________ of the boy's throat.

e The Live 8 concert was a (globe + al) ________________ event shown around the world.

f The healthy dessert was made from pure (nature + al) ________________ ingredients.

g An efficient (type + ist) ________________ doesn't need to look at the keyboard when typing.

h Large (machine + ery) ________________ was used to build the reservoir.

6 Write the oar words in alphabetical order.

________________ ________________ ________________ ________________ ________________

________________ ________________ ________________ ________________ ________________

Glido Words

7 Use the clues to complete this puzzle.

a	h				
b		h			
c			h		
d				h	
e					h
f				h	
g			h		
h		h			
i	h				

a A large four-legged animal with a mane

b A large cloth used under a blanket

c Someone who shows you to your seat

d A struggle or a battle

e To go pink in the face

f The opposite of dark

g The second of two; (not this one, the ____________)

h A sharp woody prickle on a plant

i A building for living in

An 'ant' Puzzle

8

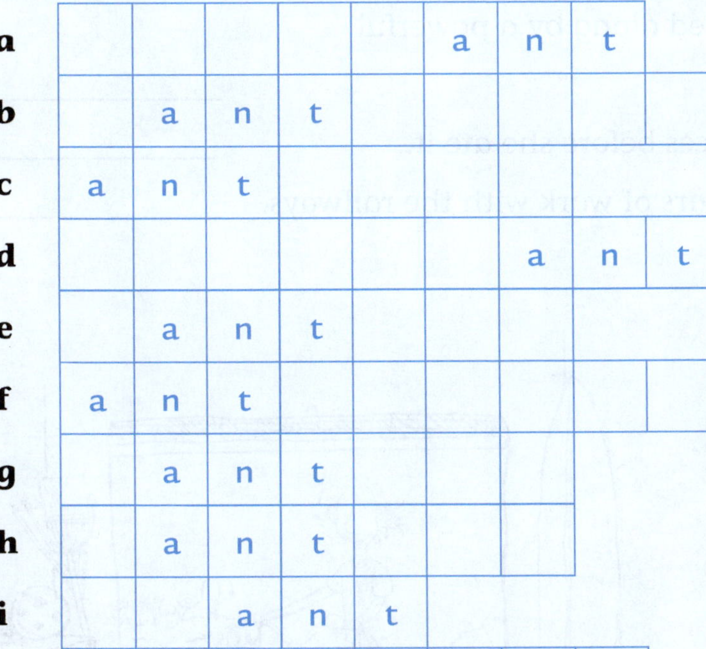

a A large animal with a trunk

b A play for children

c The feeler on the head of an insect

d Having a lot of value

e A light in a glass case

f Near the South Pole

g Bird whose tail spreads out like a fan

h A mountain lion

i Something that grows in the ground

j An animal like a deer

soft g words

engine	garage	orange	savage	agent
engineer	judge	gentle	sponge	tragic

1 **Write each of the list words in your book. Use four of the words in sentences of your own.**

2 **Unjumble the list word in each sentence.**

a It was a (icgrta) accident that resulted in the death of fifty passengers on the train. ________________

b While Lara prepared the icing for the (npsoeg), Dad whipped the cream for the filling. ________________

c Mr Johnson was asked to be a (gujde) at the Flower Show. ________________

d The lady gave the baby a (ltngee) pat on the back. ________________

e (avaSeg) winds whipped along the coastline. ________________

f The secret (gtaen) was on a dangerous mission. ________________

g After Mum washed the car she parked it in the (rggaae). ________________

h The long goods train was being pulled along by a powerful (nnegie). ________________

i Fiona cut the (enroag) into four pieces before she ate it. ________________

j The (rigennee) retired after forty years of work with the railways. ________________

3 **Complete this pattern using list words**

			g				
			a				
			r				
			a				
			g				
			e				

4 **Find all the list words in this puzzle.**

a	v	g	e	r	j	a	g	e	o
g	u	a	r	d	u	t	y	n	r
e	n	r	a	b	d	r	e	s	a
m	o	a	g	a	g	e	n	t	n
e	n	g	i	n	e	e	r	s	g
n	g	e	n	t	l	e	s	p	e
g	u	s	a	v	a	g	e	o	n
i	t	r	a	g	i	c	t	n	t
n	u	g	s	p	l	u	n	g	e
e	n	g	l	o	u	n	g	e	n

Can you find any other soft g words in the puzzle? Write them in your book.

Definitions

5 **Draw a line to match each list word with the correct definition.**

a	A person in authority in a court of law	**engine**
b	Someone who acts on behalf of another person	**engineer**
c	A machine which makes things work	**garage**
d	A sweet citrus fruit; also a colour	**judge**
e	Fierce and cruel or wild	**orange**
f	The soft yellowish skeleton of a sea animal	**gentle**
g	Someone who makes or looks after machines	**savage**
h	Quiet, soft or soothing	**sponge**
i	Describes a terrible, unhappy event	**agent**
j	A place where cars and bicycles are kept	**tragic**

6 **How many words of four letters or more can you make from the letters in the box? Each word must contain the large letter, and each letter can be used only once in each word.**

S	p	o
	e	r
t	a	m

An 'f' Puzzle

7 **a** Sum of money paid to a doctor, lawyer or private school

b Hate or violence which continues for a long time as a result of a quarrel

c A short story that teaches a moral, especially a story in which animals or objects speak

d A very serious lack of food

e To shine with an unsteady light

f A joyful celebration or a series of performances

a	f							
b	f							
c	f							
d	f							
e	f							
f	f							

Build a Word

8 **You may need to rearrange the order of the letters.**

Write down a word meaning a boy or a youth.

Add a letter to get a word meaning to guide.

Add a letter to get the sharp part of a knife.

Write down a word meaning a covering for the head.

Add a letter to get a word meaning idle talk.

Add a letter to get a word meaning a map of part of the sea showing the coastline.

Challenge words

Find the meaning of these **soft g** words and learn how to spell them.

average	suggest	generation	enrage	lounge
gymnasium	revenge	general	oblige	genuine

au words

cause	aunt	taught	daughter	auction
because	caught	naughty	slaughter	autumn

1 **Write each of the list words in your book. Use four of the words in sentences of your own.**

2 **Fill the gaps in these sentences with list words.**

a Pam is not allowed to play with her friends after school this week ________________ she was rude to her mother.

b Many people do not like the way we ________________ animals for food.

c Helen ________________ her brother how to knit.

d An inquiry was held to try to find the ________________ of the train accident.

e My ________________ and uncle are leaving on a trip to Japan next week.

f Mrs Jones has four sons and one ________________.

g Last night after school I ________________ the bus into town to buy Mum a birthday present.

h Dad doesn't have to growl at me much because usually I am not ________________ .

i My favourite season is ________________ when the leaves on deciduous trees change colour.

j Mum bought a lovely antique dresser for my bedroom at an ________________.

3 **Which list words match these definitions?**

Your father's or mother's sister ________________

A sale at which people bid against each other ________________

The killing of many persons or animals at once ________________

Something responsible for a happening ________________

The second season of the year ________________

Past tense of 'teach' ________________

For the reason that ________________

A person's female child ________________

Past tense of 'catch' ________________

Badly behaved ________________

Something to remember

When a word ends in e the e is usually kept when a suffix beginning with a consonant is added.

use—useless love—lovely

4 Add the suffix in brackets to the given word to form a new word.

hope (less)	________________	forgive (ness)	________________
strange (ly)	________________	secure (ly)	________________
price (less)	________________	idle (ness)	________________
care (ful)	________________	trouble (some)	________________
lame (ness)	________________	feeble (ness)	________________
agree (ment)	________________	polite (ly)	________________
safe (ty)	________________	shame (ful)	________________
complete (ly)	________________	amuse (ment)	________________
measure (ment)	________________	life (less)	________________
extreme (ly)	________________	rude (ness)	________________

Note these exceptions: true(ly)—truly argue(ment)—argument

5 Using the rule above add the suffix to the base word in brackets to complete each sentence.

a I love the lamingtons Mum bakes, but some I have bought from the cake shop are quite (taste + less) ________________.

b When the yacht capsized the crew was winched (safe + ly) ________________ to the rescue helicopter.

c Jake was (care + ful) ________________ not to spill any water from the bucket he was carrying.

d That painting by the Dutch master is (price + less) ________________.

e The race horse suffering from (lame + ness) ________________ had to be retired from racing.

f To our (amaze + ment) ________________the magician seemed to saw his assistant in half.

g After three days hiking the group turned and started (home + ward) ________________.

h We tied the heavy load (secure + ly) ________________to the back of the ute.

6 **Use the clues to find these au words.**

a		a	u					
b		a	u					
c		a	u					
d		a	u					
e		a	u					
f		a	u					
g		a	u					
h		a	u					
i		a	u					

a To drag along or pull

b A mistake, anything which spoils something which is otherwise good

c Another word for a large, open motorboat

d Carefulness, watchfulness

e A female child of a father and a mother

f Lived in or visited by ghosts

g A small curved plate put under a cup

h To make something happen

i To hurt badly by rough or savage treatment

History of Words

7 **Match these words with their historical clues.**

aardvark **gossip** **amphibian** **caterpillar** **daisy**

- This word literally means 'a hairy cat' and in Latin came from *catta* meaning 'cat' and *pilosus* meaning 'hairy'. ________________
- This comes from the Greek word *amphibios* meaning 'living a double life' as on land and in water. ________________
- This South African animal gets its name from two words: *aarde* meaning 'earth' and *vark* meaning 'pig'. ________________
- This plant has a little golden eye that closes at night. Sometime between 1100 and 1500, the English named it *dayeseye* which means 'day's eye'. ________________
- This word originally came from the chatting and talking among godparents which took place at a christening. ________________

Challenge words

Find the meaning of these au words and learn how to spell them.

applause exhaust pauper authentic fraud
daub nausea tarpaulin audition cauliflower

Commonly misspelt words

separate	accommodation	embarrass	signature	straight
queue	necessary	argument	thought	cupboard

1 **Write each of the list words in your book. Use four of the words in sentences of your own.**

2 **Unjumble the list words.**

uhhttog	______________	daoucpbr	______________	ssmaaberr	______________
paatesre	______________	ncomoitaacmdo	______________	uuqee	______________
yrassecen	______________	temragun	______________	ragstiht	______________

3 **Which list words match these definitions?**

A person's name in his/her own handwriting ________________

A debate or strong discussion ________________

A cabinet that has shelves ________________

To divide or put apart ________________

Without a bend ________________

A room or house for people to stay or live ________________

A line of waiting people ________________

Something that cannot be done without ________________

An idea, or, the process or action of thinking ________________

To make someone feel uncomfortable ________________

4 **Write the list words in alphabetical order.**

______________ ______________ ______________ ______________ ______________

______________ ______________ ______________ ______________ ______________

5 **Use list words to complete these sentences.**

a The footballer wrote his ________________ in the fan's autograph book.

b Whenever my friends come to our house to play my brother always tries to ________________ me.

c After ironing the sheets Dad folded them and put them away in the ________________ .

d When my great-grandmother was young she used a separator to ________________ the cream from the milk after milking the cow.

e At the ski lodge where we stayed in Canada our ________________ was very cramped.

f I ________________ the answer was right but my teacher said it was incorrect.

g Josh was very angry when the man pushed in front of us in the long ________________.

h A triangle is made up of three ________________ sides.

i It is not ________________ to wear a sunhat in the middle of winter if you live in Victoria.

j Kade and Bradley had an ________________ over whose turn it was to unload the dishwasher.

Glido Words

6 **Use the clues to complete this puzzle.**

a	t				
b		t			
c			t		
d				t	
e					t
f				t	
g			t		
h		t			
i	t				

a A path through forests, etc.

b To mark or spot something

c To fasten securely (e.g. a horse to a post)

d A territory or part of a country

e The hard outside of a loaf of bread

f Comes after the fourth

g To go into a place or an event

h To learn about a subject

i To feel with the fingers

Word Steps

7 **The end of one word begins the next word.**

a The mark left on your skin after a sore or wound has healed

b To be concerned or anxious about

c An amount of space on the ground or on a floor

d To cut and gather in crops of grain such as wheat

One or Two?

8 Add t or tt to the words below. Use a dictionary to help you if necessary.

a _______ ack	ke _______ le	si _______ e
ba _______ leship	lis _______ en	ba _______ er
vi _______ amin	weigh _______	concre _______ e
hams _______ er	hippopo _______ amus	ca _______ le
co _______ on	la _______ ch	mosqui _______ o
la _______ e	mi _______ ens	na _______ ion
mu _______ er	pe _______ icoat	po _______ ery
ra _______ ion	ra _______ le	vege _______ able

Add l or ll to these words. Use a dictionary to help you if necessary.

vani _______ a	vei _______	usua _______ y
sai _______ or	ru _______ er	a _______ most
a _______ ready	va _______ ey	sa _______ ad
ba _______ et	vi _______ age	be _______ ieve
dis _______ ike	jea _______ ous	mudd _______ e
quai _______	ski _______ ful	ski _______
si _______ kworm	unwe _______	caterpi _______ ar
comp _______ ain	fi _______ e	fo _______ y

Word Quiz EA

9 How quickly can you find these words?

a A five-letter word ending in ot _______________

b A five-letter word ending in se _______________

c A seven-letter word ending in ase _______________

d A seven-letter word ending in pet _______________

e A five-letter word ending in ng _______________

f A six-letter word ending in urt _______________

g A six-letter word ending in gue _______________

h A four-letter word ending in he _______________

Revision

1 Choose the correct word.

anwser	answer	anser	______________
hord	hoard	horrde	______________
audision	audition	aurdition	______________
oblije	aublige	oblige	______________
moden	modern	modurn	______________
transfer	transpher	tranzfer	______________
judge	jugge	gudge	______________
sentence	sentance	centence	______________
strate	straight	streight	______________
double	dooble	duble	______________
korse	coarse	coorse	______________
separate	seperate	separet	______________
tradgic	tragic	trajic	______________
cort	cauhgt	caught	______________
jeneral	genaral	general	

2 Write these words into your book and group them into word families.

butcher	police	touch
garage	taught	sentence
soar	agent	cause
answer	proper	trouble
ceiling	roar	handle
judge	hoarse	slaughter
coarse	fancy	country
daughter	orange	circle
neither	cardboard	settle

3 Find small words that are in the larger words.

courage	______________	argument	______________	castle	______________
proper	______________	butcher	______________	neither	______________
surround	______________	deliver	______________	authentic	______________
distance	______________	office	______________	place	______________
surface	______________	several	______________	retriever	______________
signature	______________	engineer	______________	garage	______________
orange	______________	slaughter	______________	cupboard	______________

Mixed Words

4 **Each group of letters contains two words. What are the words?**

Example:

```
c   a  s  tl  e         castle
↑   ↑  ↑  ↑↑  ↑
c b e a c s a t l u e s e
  ↓ ↓   ↓   ↓     ↓   ↓ ↓
  b e   c   a     u   s e   because
```

sthraandiglhte	____________	____________
hseanvderleal	____________	____________
oefxtpenert	____________	____________
sfpoanngecy	____________	____________
gcaroagueple	____________	____________
haarduwnarte	____________	____________
soofccteern	____________	____________
trporopuberle	____________	____________
dtrouablgeic	____________	____________
whdiistscleover	____________	____________
daneugiththerer	____________	____________
hcoiartsey	____________	____________
dceslertimb	____________	____________
cesiloingar	____________	____________

Jumbled Words

6 **Unjumble each word. Then write the plural for each word. The first one has been done for you.**

rneoag	orange	oranges
ucebthr	____________	____________
ingsreuta	____________	____________
cynfa	____________	____________
eltsac	____________	____________
pgsone	____________	____________
ageduhtr	____________	____________
abor	____________	____________
wernas	____________	____________
artrqeu	____________	____________
fucears	____________	____________
iieglnc	____________	____________
lericc	____________	____________

A Giant Crossword

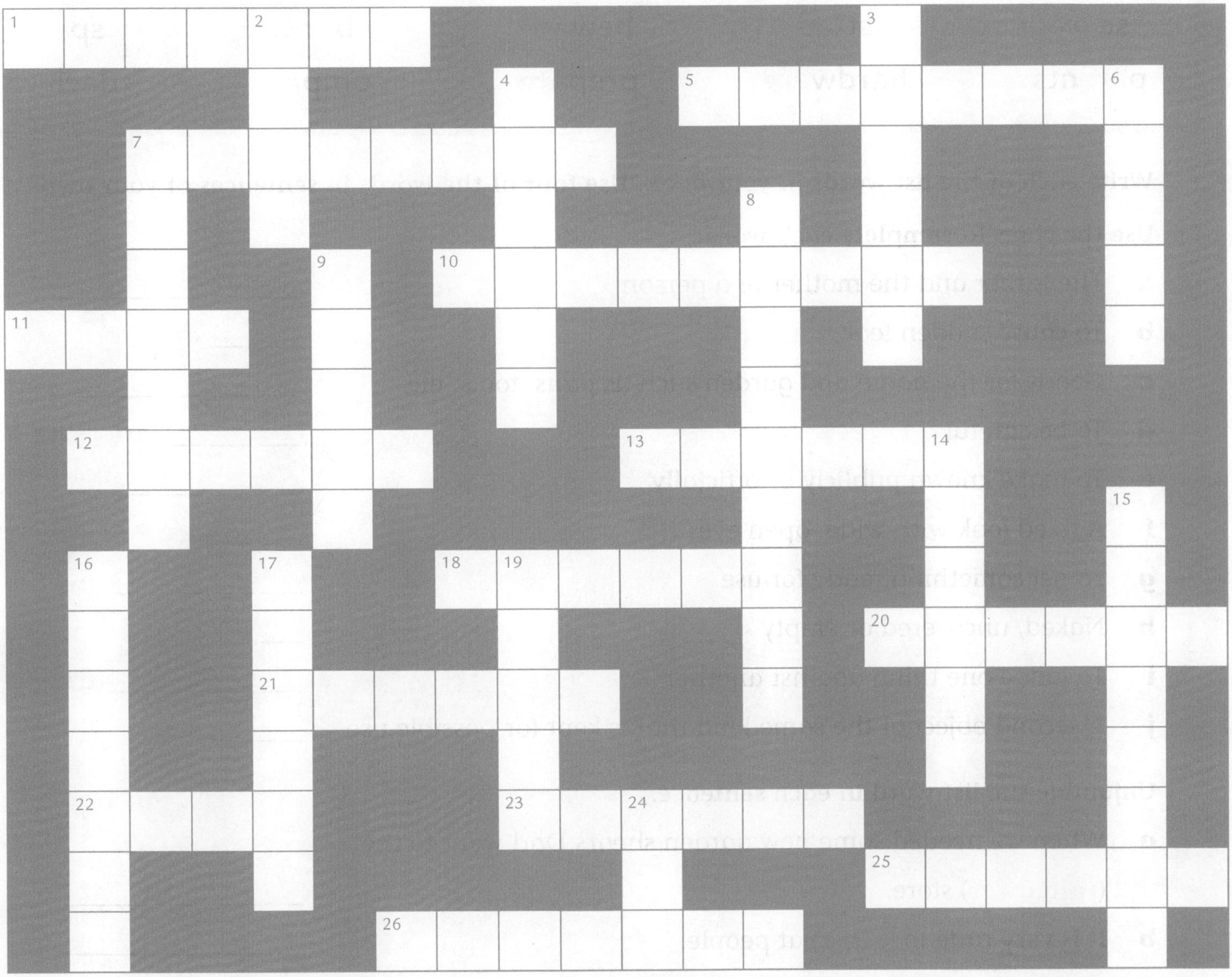

Across:

1 Bravery, lack of fear
5 Opposite of positive
7 A person who buys and uses goods and services
10 A substance that prevents and removes smells
11 A large and important town
12 Hardened into ice
13 To whiten something artificially
18 A place where cars are kept
20 To bring up mud from the bottom of a harbour or river in order to deepen it
21 Twice as much; to multiply by two
22 A male pig
23 A small, thin, furry animal that kills other small animals
25 A small curved plate under a cup
26 A watery swelling on the skin

Down:

2 Your father or mother's sister
3 A very serious lack of food
4 A large area of land with little rain
6 A stand for a picture on which an artist is working
7 One hundred years (or runs in cricket)
8 Something that is so valuable that a price cannot be put on it
9 Someone who shows you to your seat
14 Having a harsh-sounding voice
15 A person who plans and understands the making of structures and mechanical things like machines, bridges and roads
16 To shake or shiver with fear
17 Up to date
19 To permit, grant permission
24 Drawing, painting and sculpture

are words

scare	stare	beware	bare	spare
parents	hardware	prepare	compare	declare

1 **Write each of the list words in your book. Use four of the words in sentences of your own.**

2 **Use the clues to complete each word.**

a The father and the mother of a person ___ are ___ ___ ___

b To cause sudden fear ___ ___ are

c Goods for the home and garden such as pans, tools, etc. ___ ___ ___ ___ ___ are

d To be careful ___ ___ ___ are

e To make known publicly or officially ___ ___ ___ ___ are

f A fixed look with wide, open eyes ___ ___ are

g To get something ready for use ___ ___ ___ ___ are

h Naked, uncovered or empty ___ are

i To judge one thing against another ___ ___ ___ ___ are

j A second object of the same kind that is kept for possible use ___ ___ are

3 **Unjumble the list word in each sentence.**

a When we needed some new garden shears Dad went to the (rahadwer) store. ________________

b It is very rude to (atser) at people. ________________

c Cathy got quite a (rcsae) when her brother crept up behind her. ________________

d The oak tree looked very (eabr) after the autumn leaves had blown away. ________________

e The sign said '(eeBwar) of the dog'. ________________

f Stephanie likes to help her mother (arpeper) the meat sauce for the spaghetti. ________________

g I love my (erapnts). ________________

h Tinned soup just doesn't (mcoapre) with homemade soup. ________________

i The traveller had nothing to (deeclar) at customs. ________________

4 **Which list word has:**

a black, sticky substance? ______________

a smaller word which is opposite to soft? ______________

something you might have after a wound has healed? ______________

a smaller word which is the opposite of peace? ______________

an iron rod? ______________

The golfing term par means equal or level. Which four list words contain the smaller word par? ______________ ______________ ______________ ______________

5 **Write the list words in alphabetical order.**

______________ ______________ ______________ ______________ ______________

______________ ______________ ______________ ______________ ______________

6 **What list words when put in the spaces make three-letter words reading across?**

i		e
c		d
i		p
a		e
c		n
a		e
t		n

a		e
r		n
a		e
p		n
a		t
a		e
a		k

e		b
t		a
t		o
s		t
o		e
s		a

a		k
a		e
b		t
a		e
b		t

a		h
a		e
r		w
a		t
p		n

A 'g' Puzzle

7 **a** A small two-wheeled carriage pulled by a horse

b A round piece of metal hanging from a frame which when struck gives a deep ringing sound

c To take care of horses, especially by rubbing, brushing and cleaning

d A six-stringed musical instrument larger than a violin

e Rubbish or refuse

f Masses of ice which move very slowly down mountain valleys

a	g							
b	g							
c	g							
d	g							
e	g							
f	g							

Hidden Words

8 **Which six list words are hidden here? Each word is in two parts.**

ents	ware	par
pare	de	com
be	pare	clare
hard	pre	ware

__________ __________ __________ __________ __________ __________

Contractions

9 **Draw lines to match the contractions in List A with the correct words in List B.**

List A	List B
wouldn't	I have
couldn't	you would
who's	would not
I've	they have
I'll	there is
you'd	did not
there's	who is
didn't	she will
she'll	I will
they've	could not

tch words

latch	stretch	batch	stretcher	clutch
stitch	fetch	pitch	dispatch	hutch

1 **Write each of the list words in your book. Use four of the words in sentences of your own.**

2 **Draw a line to match each definition with the correct list word.**

latch	**a**	A covered frame on which a sick person can be carried lying down
stitch	**b**	The degree of highness or lowness of a musical note
clutch	**c**	A metal fastening for a door or gate
stretch	**d**	A group or a quantity
fetch	**e**	A movement of a needle and thread into cloth at one point and out at another
batch	**f**	To send off things such as letters and parcels
hutch	**g**	To make or become wider or longer
stretcher	**h**	To go and get, and bring back
pitch	**i**	To grasp or snatch
dispatch	**j**	A pen for rabbits

3 **Arrange these groups of tch words in alphabetical order.**

a	latch	batch	catch	hatch	patch
	______	______	______	______	______
b	match	clutch	watch	fetch	pitch
	______	______	______	______	______
c	butcher	kitchen	dispatch	Dutch	witch
	______	______	______	______	______
d	stitch	stretch	snatch	scratch	stretcher
	______	______	______	______	______
e	hutch	watch	wretched	satchel	latch
	______	______	______	______	______

Compound Words

Something to remember

Compound words are made when two smaller words are put together to make a larger word.

For example: every + body = everybody hall + way = hallway

With compound words, no letters are left out.

4 Match a word from List A with a word from List B to make a compound word.

List A	List B	Compound Words
sun	stand	________________
lip	way	________________
grand	bow	________________
ship	set	________________
shell	stick	________________
arm	fish	________________
high	day	________________
day	chair	________________
birth	dream	________________
rain	wreck	________________

5 Find two words in each sentence that can be joined to make a compound word.

a I think I will type an email to my favourite writer. ________________

b In the sun the flower bloomed. ________________

c We heard the thunder during the wild storm. ________________

d During my life I hope to be a saver not a big spender. ________________

e The boy with ginger hair stole the loaf of bread. ________________

f My candle is dark blue but yours is light blue. ________________

g Dad had to stop driving so we could watch the parade. ________________

h Against the wall blew all the paper. ________________

i On the table was a large cloth. ________________

j There was a large letter J written on the box. ________________

Word Puzzle

6 **How many words of four letters or more can you make from the letters in the box? Each word must contain the large letter, and each letter can be used only once in each word.**

t	c	h
	s	a
c	r	o

________________ ________________ ________________ ________________

________________ ________________ ________________ ________________

________________ ________________ ________________ ________________

________________ ________________ ________________ ________________

Glido Words

7 **Use the clues to complete this puzzle.**

a	a				
b		a			
c			a		
d				a	
e					a
f				a	
g			a		
h		a			
i	a				

a Joint connecting the foot and leg

b A piece of material to cover a hole

c Soft white limestone used for drawing

d White substance that makes foods sweet

e A play in which words are sung

f Bright; plain to see

g A breakable, see-through material

h A piece of furniture with four legs

i Living; not dead

Sentences

8 **Fill each gap with a word from the list.**

a The baker made a large ________________ of scones.

b All that running gave me a ________________ in my side.

c Make sure the ________________ on the door is secure.

d After the accident he was carried off on a ________________.

e I wonder if this material will ________________.

f Our choir leader listened to the tune and ________________ of our voices.

g The farmer got the dogs to ________________ the sheep.

h We will need to ________________ that report immediately to the Field Commander.

se words

sense	else	lose	choose	rouse
surprise	please	loose	tease	excuse

1 **Write each of the list words in your book. Use four of the words in sentences of your own.**

2 **Choose the correct list word to complete each sentence.**

a Would you (tease, please) help me with my homework? ____________

b Her hair hung (lose, loose) over her shoulders. ____________

c Don't (tease, please) the cat or it will scratch you. ____________

d There is no (surprise, sense) in crying over spilt milk. ____________

e Which dress did the girl (choose, else)? ____________

f Don't (lose, loose) your way in the storm. ____________

g Michelle was talking in class when she should have been doing something (sense, else). ____________

h To my great (sense, surprise) there was a goat walking along the main street of the shopping centre. ____________

i We had to (rouse, sense) Dad when he fell fast asleep on the couch. ____________

j Brodie had no (sense, excuse) for not doing his maths homework. ____________

What Am I?

3 **Use the clues to find the list word.**

My first letter is in *holster* and also in *wasp*.

My second letter is in *suspect* and also in *rhubarb*.

My third letter is in *crush* but not in *cushion*.

My fourth letter is in *ample* but not in *amble*.

My fifth letter is in *floor* and also in *mixture*.

My sixth letter is in *script* and also in *yield*.

My seventh letter is in *sawn* but not in *yawn*.

My last letter is in *precede* and also in *alone*.

What am I? ____________

4 **Complete this clueless crossword puzzle by using these se words. Start with surprise.**

lose	horse	please	moose	sense	tease	else
cheese	loose	house	surprise	mouse	excuse	nurse

Glido Words

5 **Use the clues to complete this puzzle.**

a	n				
b		n			
c			n		
d				n	
e					n
f				n	
g			n		
h		n			
i	n				

a Not ever, not at any time

b Your father's or mother's brother

c To be affected by a great fear

d To use money, to use up

e The colour of most leaves

f To crush to a powder

g Variety; practice ground for shooting

h Someone who is hostile or fights against you

i A person trained to help doctors

6 **Write the list words in alphabetical order.**

______ ______ ______ ______ ______

______ ______ ______ ______ ______

Word Quiz (EA)

7 **How quickly can you find these words?**

a A nine-letter word ending in her ______

b A nine-letter word ending in ent ______

c A seven-letter word ending in ess ______

d An eight-letter word ending in eer ______

e A six-letter word ending in ius ______

f A six-letter word ending in nge ______

g A seven-letter word ending in ach ______

h A six-letter word ending in hor ______

i An eight-letter word ending in der ______

j A six-letter word ending in ouch ______

Anagrams (EA)

An anagram is what you get when you change the order of letters in a word to make a new word.

For example: meat—tame

8 **a** Change rates into something people have when they cry. ______

b Change hated into the end of life. ______

c Change dance into beaten or hit with a stick. ______

d Change read into very expensive. ______

e Change loots into something we sit on. ______

f Change thing into the time of day when the stars can be seen in the sky. ______

g Change charm into the third month of the year. ______

h Change peels into something we do at night. ______

ph words

graph	telephone	nephew	orphan	telegraph
elephant	photograph	autograph	alphabet	atmosphere

1 **Write each of the list words in your book. Use four of the words in sentences of your own.**

Alphabetical Order

2 **Arrange these groups of ph words into alphabetical order.**

a	nephew	atmosphere	elephant	orphan	graph
	______	______	______	______	______
b	telegraph	photograph	sphere	alphabet	telephone
	______	______	______	______	______
c	autograph	biography	geography	atmosphere	pamphlet
	______	______	______	______	______
d	pheasant	phonics	phrase	physical	phantom
	______	______	______	______	______

3 **Complete each sentence with a list word.**

a On Saturday Bruce took his niece and ________________ to the movies.

b Our neighbours, Mr and Mrs Watson, have adopted an ________________ from South Korea.

c I knew the complete ________________ from A to Z before I started school.

d For maths we had to make a ________________ showing what months everyone in the class had their birthdays in.

e It is much easier to get a perfect ________________ using a digital camera.

f My favourite cricketer, Adam Gilchrist, signed his name in my ________________ book.

g We changed our Internet to broadband because, before that, we couldn't use our computer and the ________________ at the same time.

h The African ________________ has large ears and is usually a bigger animal than the Indian ________________.

Something to remember

If a word ends in a y with a consonant before the y, then when a suffix is added, the y is changed to an i. For example: merry—merriment

Note: This does not apply if the suffix begins with i.

4 Add the suffix in brackets to the given word to form a new word.

beauty (ful) ________________

easy (est) ________________

lonely (ness) ________________

weary (ness) ________________

duty (ful) ________________

tidy (ness) ________________

fury (ous) ________________

happy (ness) ________________

bury (al) ________________

plenty (ful) ________________

glory (ous) ________________

silly (ness) ________________

noisy (est) ________________

mystery (ous) ________________

5 Using the rule above, add the suffix to the base word in brackets to complete the sentences.

a Towards the end of the long hike we trudged (weary + ly) ________________ back to our base camp.

b Niall was given a merit certificate for being a very (rely + able) ________________ monitor.

c Saschelle (easy + ly) ________________ got through the challenge ropes course at our school camp.

d Dad was (fury + ous) ________________ when his boss told him he would have to work on Saturday.

e The old crystal vase on display at the museum was (beauty + ful) ________________.

Hidden Words

6 Which four list words are hidden here? Each word is in three parts.

al	mos	phant
phone	el	phere
bet	tel	pha
e	e	at

________________ ________________

________________ ________________

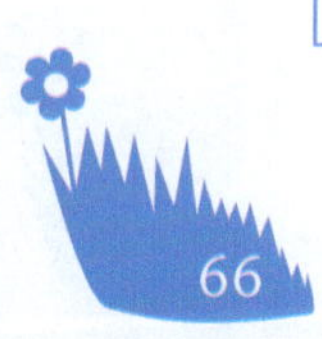

Definitions

7 **Circle the correct definition to go with the list word.**

a An **autograph** is

- a vehicle displaying pictures
- the story of a person's life written by him or herself
- a person's own signature
- a graph showing the number of cars owned in Australia.

b An **orphan** is

- a person who plays the organ
- a bulb-like vegetable with a strong smell and flavour
- a large musical instrument with a keyboard
- a child whose mother and father are both dead.

c A **telegraph** is

- a way to send messages quickly by electricity
- an instrument that brings pictures through the air
- an instrument you look through to see the stars
- a graph showing the number of television sets owned in New Zealand.

d **Atmosphere** is

- a scientist who studies the stars
- the air that is around the earth
- a person who studies cycles of planets
- a round ball or sphere.

e A **nephew** is

- the son of a brother or sister
- the child of your aunt or uncle
- the brother of your mother or father
- a son of the same parents.

Challenge words

Find the meaning of these **ph** words and learn how to spell them.

pheasant	philosopher	phlegm	pharmacy	physical
physician	phrase	phlox	phantom	epitaph

eigh words

neighbour	weight	eight	eighty
weigh	freight	eighteen	neigh

1 **Write each of the list words in your book. Use four of the words in sentences of your own.**

2 **Complete these sentences with words from the list.**

a My grandfather is ________________ years old and often tells me stories about the Second World War.

b The butcher had to ________________ the meat to see how much it would cost.

c The ________________ of the full bag of potatoes was too much for me to lift.

d My brother Dale, who is ________________, is ten years older than my cousin Ray, who is ________________.

e At the railway yards the goods train was being loaded with ________________ .

f The sound a horse makes is called a ________________.

g Our next door ________________ broke his ankle yesterday when he slipped on a banana peel.

3 **Can you find all of the list words in this puzzle?**

e	s	n	e	e	z	e	p
i	w	e	i	g	h	t	l
g	e	i	g	h	t	y	o
h	i	g	h	v	n	a	e
t	g	h	t	u	e	t	s
e	h	b	y	n	i	b	c
e	f	o	e	i	g	h	t
n	s	u	t	p	h	o	n
r	f	r	e	i	g	h	t

4 Fill in the blanks with the list words that match these definitions.

A number made by adding eight and ten ________________

The noise made by a horse ________________

A cargo or trainload ________________

To find how heavy something is ________________

Someone who lives nearby ________________

The number between seven and nine ________________

Heaviness; a load or burden ________________

Eight times ten ________________

5 Write the list words in alphabetical order.

______________ ______________ ______________ ______________

______________ ______________ ______________ ______________

Glido Words

6 Use the clues to complete this puzzle.

a	n				
b		n			
c			n		
d				n	
e					n
f				n	
g			n		
h		n			
i	n				

a Of high birth or rank

b To come or go into a place

c A long seat or a work-table

d To appear often (like a ghost)

e Sharp, woody prickle on some plants

f To mix together; a mixture

g Something we use to hear, taste, touch

h A vegetable with a strong smell

i A direction; opposite of south

More Contractions

7 **Draw lines to match the contractions in List A with the words in List B. Go back to page 36 if you're not sure what contractions are.**

List A	List B
I'd	we will
you're	is not
we'll	you will
isn't	I would
we've	he would
needn't	we would
you'll	need not
can't	you are
we'd	cannot
he'd	we have

Which is Correct?

8 **Use these letter groups to complete each word.**

ar er or ur

terr ___ ___	p___ ___ snip	corn___ ___
simil___ ___	vineg ___ ___	err ___ ___
ch___ ___ ch	blist ___ ___	doll ___ ___
burgl ___ ___	p ___ ___ se	ch ___ ___ n
oyst ___ ___	emper ___ ___	sw ___ ___ e
timb ___ ___	coll ___ ___	kang ___ ___ oo

Half an Animal

9 **In this puzzle find the names of the creatures. All have two-syllable names and the clue tells you something about half of each animal's name.**

a The last half of this bird is a neat line of things side by side. ________________

b The first half of this creature is a perch or branch on which birds settle at night. ________________

c The last half of this bird means to decay. ________________

d The last half of this creature can be used in a game of cricket. ________________

igh words

delight	alight	height	plight
tight	knight	slight	blight

1 Write each of the list words in your book. Use each one in a sentence of your own.

2 Complete this clueless crossword puzzle by using these **igh** words. Start with **frighten**.

tight tighten sigh blight frighten airtight
right slight flight knight height delight

	f		i	g	h								
	r									i	g	h	
	i			i	g	h			i				i
	g								g				g
	h		i	g	h				h		i		h
	t									i	g	h	
	e		i	g	h						h		
	n												
			i	g	h								
									i	g	h		

Alphabetical Order

3 Arrange these groups of **igh** words into alphabetical order.

a sigh right frighten delight blight

_______ _______ _______ _______ _______

b thigh fight slight plight tighten

_______ _______ _______ _______ _______

c high height bright flight fright

_______ _______ _______ _______ _______

d alight lighten knight light sight

_______ _______ _______ _______ _______

'i' before 'e'

Something to remember

Everyone knows the spelling rule: i before e, except after c. This rule works for most of our words, for example:

thief	yield	fierce
deceive	receive	perceive

But there are exceptions such as veil, rein and beige (which all have an ay sound); reign, sovereign and foreign (which all have a g after the ei) and height and sleight (which rhyme with ite).

So someone extended the rule to: i before e,

Except after c and before g
Or when sounded like a
As in 'neighbour' or 'weigh'
Or when sounded like 'ite'
As in 'height' or 'sleight'

This extended rule now covers most of our words, but there are still a few exceptions such as heifer, weird and seize.

4 Using the extended 'i-e' rule above, complete these words by adding ie or ei.

n ___ ___ ghbour	h ___ ___ ght	repl ___ ___ d
bel ___ ___ f	w ___ ___ ght	fr ___ ___ ze
conc ___ ___ t	c ___ ___ ling	w ___ ___ ld
handkerch ___ ___ f	bes ___ ___ ge	dec ___ ___ ve

5 Use these exceptions to the extended rule in sentences of your own.

heifer ____

weird ____

seize ____

Definitions

6 **Circle the correct definition to go with the list word.**

a A knight is

- a robber on horseback who held up travellers on the road
- the time between sunset and sunrise when the sky is dark
- a nobleman who used to dress in armour and fight for his king
- a toy made of paper or cloth on light wood.

b A blight is

- a curve in the coastline
- a disease of plants caused by parasites
- a bundle of sticks
- someone who has to see that rules are obeyed in games and sports.

c Slight means

- small in quantity; slim or slender
- rain mixed with snow or hail
- to give off bright flashes of light
- not very clear or sure.

d Tight means

- not properly fastened
- to linger; to dawdle
- a feeling of being glad and happy when you are enjoying yourself
- close-fitting or closely packed.

e A light means

- something you turn on so that you can see in the dark
- in flames; burning
- to make less heavy or less dark
- a sudden bright flash in the sky when there is a thunderstorm.

f Plight means

- a fold in cloth, pressed or stitched down to keep it in place
- an unhappy state or condition
- rather fat and well-rounded
- a small, light purse.

oy words

voyage enjoy destroy enjoyment
joyful employ oyster employment

1 **Write each of the list words in your book. Use four of the words in sentences of your own.**

2 **Complete these sentences using list words.**

a In Australia and New Zealand we can ________________ some of the world's most beautiful scenery.

b The guests ate the fine meal with ________________.

c I have only ever eaten one ________________ and it made me feel ill.

d Captain Cook made a historic ________________ in the *Endeavour*.

e When the new mill is built it will ________________ three hundred workers.

f The soldiers' mission was to ________________ the enemy's headquarters.

g The student was looking for ________________ during the holidays.

h The birth of the baby was a ________________ event.

3 Which three list words end in oy? ______________ ______________ ______________

Which list word begins with oy? ______________

Which two list words end in ment? ______________ ______________

Which list word contains a smaller word meaning length of life? ______________

Which list word ends with the suffix ful? ______________

4 **Write the list words in alphabetical order.**

______________ ______________ ______________ ______________

______________ ______________ ______________ ______________

5 **Next to each list word, write the number of syllables it contains.**

employ ☐	destroy ☐	enjoyment ☐
voyage ☐	oyster ☐	enjoy ☐
joyful ☐	employment ☐	

6 **Match the list word to the definition.**

To give work to ______________

To get joy from ______________

A kind of shellfish ______________

To break down, ruin or kill ______________

A journey by water ______________

An extension of 'enjoy' ______________

Full of delight and gladness ______________

Regular occupation or being employed ______________

Did You Know?

7 **The list word destroy (and destruction) comes from the Latin *de* meaning down and *struere* meaning 'to build'. Therefore it means to undo construction.**

Building Words

8 **Add a letter at the beginning and a letter at the end of each of the following groups of letters to form six-letter words. The first letters must all be the same and the final letters when reading downwards spell the name of a soldier who guards a palace gate.**

___ HEAR ___

___ IMPL ___

___ ALMO ___

___ ECRE ___

___ HOWE ___

___ AFET ___

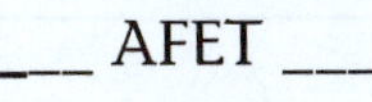

Spell a Word Backwards 

9 **Here are two sets of clues. Find the first answer, spell it backwards and you will have the second answer. For example the answer to a (i) is stink and a (ii) knits.**

a (i) To smell unpleasant stink

(ii) Weaves with needles and wool knits

b (i) The rise and fall of the sea ______________

(ii) To prepare for publication ______________

c (i) A snare ______________

(ii) A portion ______________

d (i) A person suffering from leprosy ______________

(ii) Opposite of attract ______________

e (i) Dried wheat stalks ______________

(ii) Small hard lumps on the skin ______________

f (i) The hour of the day ______________

(ii) To give or send out ______________

T-sers EA

10 **Unjumble the letters.**

a Add t to great and get a mark or object to be aimed at in shooting and archery. ______________

b Add t to are and get a drop of liquid that comes from your eye when you cry. ______________

c Add t to eels and get a very strong metal made from iron. ______________

d Add t to pea and get a narrow strip of strong cloth used for tying or binding. ______________

e Add t to fee and get a large outdoor money-raising activity. ______________

f Add t to base and get a word meaning an animal. ______________

g Add t to liar and get a track or path. ______________

h Add t to shone and get a word meaning truthful and trustworthy. ______________

i Add t to ache and get a word meaning to explain to someone how to do something. ______________

j Add t to raw and get a small hard lump on the skin. ______________

The Great Barrier Reef

coral	shellfish	tourists	marine	sanctuary
submerged	biologists	Queensland	crustaceans	cays

1 **Write each of the list words in your book. Use four of the words in sentences of your own.**

2 **Complete this passage about the Great Barrier Reef by unjumbling the list words.**

The Great Barrier Reef is the largest (aocrl) ________________ structure in the world and is about 15 000 years old. It covers an area of over 200 000 square kilometres off the (nuelsQenad) ________________ coast. It is a wildlife (yatcnsaur) ________________, one of the largest in the world, and attracts hundreds of thousands of (riuottss) ________________ every year.

There are about 200 coral islands called (yacs) ________________ on the Great Barrier Reef, which are usually flat and barren. Some, such as Heron Island and Green Island, rise to a height of twenty metres. The highest islands are the peaks of (dbeesumrg) ________________ mountains that were once part of the Australian mainland.

The Great Barrier Reef is famous for its delicate and brilliantly coloured (arnmie) ________________ life. It has starfish, coral trout, black marlin, green turtles, (sctsrcunaae) ________________, manta rays and sunfish. It also has some of the world's largest (siehsllfh) ________________, including the giant clam, which can weigh more than 225 kilograms.

Recently, marine (sslooibgit) ________________ have become concerned with the damage being caused to live coral on the Great Barrier Reef.

3 **Match the list words to these definitions.**

A state of Australia ________________

A sea animal with a shell ________________

Scientists who study animals and plants ________________

Coral islands (the answer is sometimes pronounced as 'keys') ________________

Hard substance secreted by small sea creatures ________________

People who travel for pleasure ________________

Concerning the sea ________________

A type of sea animal usually with a hard shell and numerous jointed legs ________________

Prefixes

Something to remember

A **prefix** is a group of letters that comes before a base word to make a new word.
Often, it will change the meaning of the word.

For example: base word—happy prefix—un new word—unhappy

The prefix usually has a specific meaning. For example, the prefix un means not or the reverse of.
So unhappy means not happy.

4 Write the given prefix in front of each of the base words. Then use one of the new words in a sentence of your own.

il (meaning 'not')

______ legal ______ logical ______ legible

Sentence: ______________________________

auto (meaning 'self')

______ graph ______ biography ______ matic

Sentence: ______________________________

bi (meaning 'two')

______ cycle ______ plane ______ sect

Sentence: ______________________________

dis (meaning 'not, apart from')

______ obey ______ appear ______ agree

Sentence: ______________________________

re (meaning 'again, back')

______ place ______ assure ______ pay

Sentence: ______________________________

5 Use the prefixes in the box to place before the base words to make new words.

semi	tri	un	trans	anti	extra	in	im

______________plant ______________climax ______________circle

_______________mature _______________complete _______________angle

_______________ordinary _______________even _______________clear

_______________clockwise _______________sensory _______________perfect

_______________dependent _______________port _______________cycle

Compound Words

The list word 'shellfish' is a compound word (**shell + fish**).

6 **Match a word from List A with a word from List B to make a compound word.**

List A	List B	Compound Word
any	keeper	_______________
some	cloth	_______________
head	thing	_______________
stop	layer	_______________
wall	watch	_______________
shop	box	_______________
cup	times	_______________
table	paper	_______________
letter	board	_______________
brick	light	_______________

Great Barrier Reef Words

7 **Here are some more Great Barrier Reef words. Learn how to spell them and make sure you know what they are. Write all of the words into your own book. Then choose five of the words to use in sentences of your own.**

barrier	fauna	wildlife
sea-urchins	flora	species
crayfish	herons	anemone
gannets	marlin	invertebrates
beche-de-mer	gulf	
terns	Gladstone	

a ____

b ____

c ____

d ____

e ____

Revision

1 Choose the correct word.

streatch	stretch	strectch	______________
choose	chouse	chows	______________
suprise	surprize	surprise	______________
graph	graf	groffe	______________
eighteen	ateteen	eighten	______________
knite	knight	knihgt	______________
orfan	aurphan	orphan	______________
oyster	oister	oystar	______________
sense	sence	cense	______________
alpherbet	alphabet	alferbet	______________
marine	maryne	mareene	______________
weigh	wiegh	wey	______________
nefew	nepheu	nephew	______________
stitch	stich	stetch	______________
alite	alight	elyte	______________

2 Write these words into your book and group them into word families.

parents	pitch	stare
choose	slight	freight
lose	beware	elephant
blight	employment	loose
knight	telegraph	tease
declare	weigh	destroy
delight	stretcher	dispatch
latch	atmosphere	please
oyster	voyage	neighbour

3 Find small words that are in the larger words.

freight	______________	enjoyment	______________	tease	______________
Queensland	______________	voyage	______________	orphan	______________
photograph	______________	dispatch	______________	atmosphere	______________
height	______________	please	______________	delight	______________
stretcher	______________	tourists	______________	batch	______________

Mixed Words

4 Each group of letters contains two words. What are the words?

Example:

```
f   e t  c  h        fetch
↑   ↑ ↑  ↑  ↑
f s e e t n c s h e
  ↓ ↓     ↓   ↓   ↓
  s e     n   s   e  sense
```

snterepthceherw	____________	____________
solysitghert	____________	____________
bcrehoaosthee	____________	____________
ppihottocgrhaph	____________	____________
tmeilalisoen	____________	____________
ewaegiglhe	____________	____________
pnleeiagshe	____________	____________
djwoyeflull	____________	____________
efmepltoycmehnt	____________	____________
voincyreagasee	____________	____________
nweiicghkbeoutr	____________	____________
kalniloghwt	____________	____________

Jumbled Words

5 Unjumble each word. Then write the plural for each word. The first one has been done for you.

phagr	graph	graphs
tteerrsch	____________	____________
spurrsei	____________	____________
weephn	____________	____________
roginehbu	____________	____________
hctab	____________	____________
pcisdath	____________	____________
tgnkih	____________	____________
norahp	____________	____________
eayovg	____________	____________
eryost	____________	____________
rutasncay	____________	____________
igneh	____________	____________

A Giant Word Search

6 **How many words can you find in this giant word search? The words go across the page or down the page. Colour in the words as you find them.**

E	P	E	A	C	E	F	A	U	S	M	T
I	A	U	T	O	G	R	A	P	H	I	D
G	L	D	M	R	A	E	L	L	I	L	E
H	I	E	O	A	T	I	P	M	E	L	L
T	G	S	S	E	I	G	H	T	Y	I	I
E	H	T	P	L	G	H	A	B	O	O	G
E	T	R	H	U	H	T	B	R	N	N	H
N	E	O	E	W	T	G	E	I	G	H	T
E	C	Y	R	E	E	L	T	O	N	G	H
I	O	N	E	I	G	H	B	O	U	R	G
E	L	S	E	G	R	O	C	K	E	T	H
B	L	I	G	H	T	J	O	Y	F	U	L
D	A	T	D	B	C	R	E	A	O	P	S
W	R	N	I	A	Y	S	K	U	L	L	U
E	X	N	S	T	R	E	T	C	H	E	R
L	I	S	P	C	C	N	E	A	E	A	P
L	K	T	A	H	Z	S	A	L	I	S	R
Y	P	I	T	C	H	E	S	L	G	E	I
F	E	T	C	H	A	N	E	O	H	D	S
S	L	C	H	O	O	S	E	W	T	R	E
W	E	H	K	N	I	G	H	T	E	U	W
A	P	H	O	T	O	G	R	A	P	H	S
L	H	S	R	E	D	R	I	L	L	U	W
L	A	E	P	L	I	G	H	T	N	D	E
O	N	A	H	E	A	L	O	O	S	E	I
W	T	S	A	G	Y	A	G	N	J	U	G
N	E	O	N	R	S	T	R	E	T	C	H
E	A	N	C	A	L	C	A	I	E	V	T
A	G	M	I	P	I	H	P	G	L	A	R
C	E	A	R	H	G	L	H	H	E	L	A
B	R	E	A	T	H	E	A	Y	P	L	E
L	O	S	E	C	T	N	E	P	H	E	W
E	E	I	N	C	R	A	M	E	O	Y	R
A	O	N	J	E	A	G	L	E	N	M	C
S	F	I	O	Y	S	T	E	R	E	I	F
H	V	O	Y	A	G	E	M	P	L	O	Y

ure words

nature	picture	capture	measure	figure
furniture	pleasure	temperature	literature	manufacture

1 Write each of the list words in your book. Use four of the words in sentences of your own.

2 Unjumble the list word in each sentence.

a *The Wind in the Willows* is one of the classics of children's (eretliratu). ____________

b He named a (ifruge) that was much more than we could pay. ____________

c The old house contained a lot of antique (uurirfnte). ____________

d I'd like to leave the city and discover (utnare) in the countryside. ____________

e The factory was built to (namafucurte) car engines. ____________

f Did you (eermasu) the windows before buying the curtains? ____________

g The gift gave the child a great deal of (lspueear). ____________

h This is a (ricptue) of the view of Mt Feathertop. ____________

i The (mteptreraue) dropped quickly once the cool change arrived. ____________

j Captain Ahab tried desperately to (erutpac) the white whale. ____________

What Am I?

3 Use the clues to find this list word.

My first letter is in *spirit* and also in *opaque*.

My second letter is in *mist* but not in *most*.

My third letter is in *furnace* and also in *lick*.

My fourth letter is in *light* and *hutch* and *betray*.

My fifth letter is in *bury* but not in *berry*.

My sixth letter is in *steer* and also in *rigid*.

My last letter is in *office* but not in *official*.

What am I? ________________

Antonyms

Something to remember

Antonyms are words that are opposite in meaning. For example:

noisy—quiet slow—fast

4 Look at each word in the first column. Then, from the group of words opposite it, circle the word that is its antonym or opposite in meaning.

unique	rare, unusual, common
waste	waist, conserve, spoil
fertile	barren, soil, manure
arrive	enter, leave, stay
modern	new, trendy, ancient
captivity	jailed, freedom, cell
reveal	show, display, conceal
familiar	unfamiliar, known, common
solid	dense, thick, hollow
powerful	weak, strong, gigantic

5 Complete these sentences by using antonyms for the coloured words.

a The river was shallow in summer, but very _________________ after the winter rains.

b The defendant was found guilty at the first trial, but when it went to the Appeals Court he was found to be _________________.

c Mike's attendance at football training is very regular, but Fraser's is very _________________.

d Ruby's bedroom is always tidy but Reegan's is so _________________!

e The lovely weather soon turned _________________ when the storm blew in and it started to rain.

f It was just as difficult to descend the steep mountain slope as it was to _________________ it.

g Water is liquid but ice, which is only frozen water, is _________________.

h The windows in our lounge are transparent but those in the bathroom are _________________ .

6 **Complete this pattern using list words.**

			p							
			l							
			a							
			n							
			e							
			t							

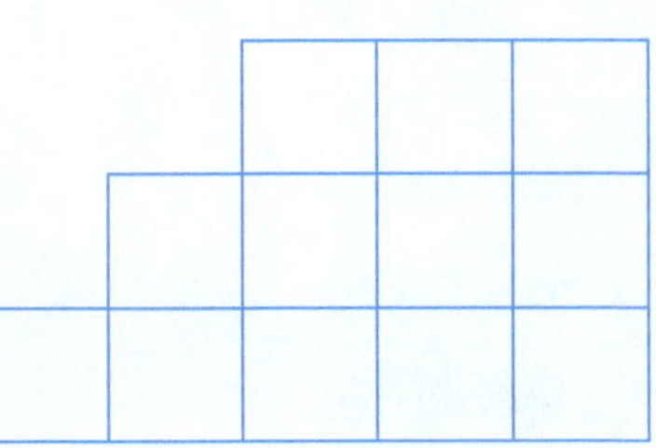

Build a Word

7 **Write down a word that means not feeling very well.**

Add a letter and get a word for tablet.

Add another letter to get a word for tip over (especially liquids).

Letter Subtraction

FUN

8 **Start with this nine-letter word:** **startling**

a Subtract one letter to get a word meaning a common type of bird. ___ ___ ___ ___ ___ ___ ___ ___

b Subtract one letter and get a word meaning looking with a long, fixed look. ___ ___ ___ ___ ___ ___ ___

c Subtract one letter and get a word meaning thin cord. ___ ___ ___ ___ ___ ___

d Subtract one letter and get a word meaning to prick and cause a sharp pain. ___ ___ ___ ___ ___

e Subtract one letter and get a word meaning to produce musical sounds with the voice. ___ ___ ___ ___

f Subtract one letter and get a word meaning the breaking of a law regarded as holy. ___ ___ ___

g Subtract one letter and get a word which can mean fashionable. ___ ___

h Subtract one letter and what are you left with? ___

or words

mirror	horror	decorate	corridor	tractor
author	conductor	junior	monitor	equator

1 **Write each of the list words in your book. Use four of the words in sentences of your own.**

Definitions

2 **Draw a line to match each definition with the correct list word.**

mirror	**a**	A heavy motor with wheels that pulls things along
author	**b**	A piece of glass with something behind it so that you can see yourself and not through the glass
horror	**c**	A pupil chosen by the teacher to help in certain ways
conductor	**d**	To make something look pretty
decorate	**e**	A long narrow passage with rooms leading off it
corridor	**f**	A person who stands in front of an orchestra and beats time
tractor	**g**	An imaginary line around the middle of the earth's surface
equator	**h**	The writer of a book, play or article
monitor	**i**	Someone who is younger or less important than others
junior	**j**	A very great fear or loathing

Hidden Words

3 **Which four list words are hidden here? Each word is in three parts.**

ate	dor	corr
or	con	tor
e	i	or
dec	duct	qua

________________ ________________

________________ ________________

4 Complete these sentences using the list words.

a I love to ________________ the Christmas tree the week before Christmas.

b If you cross the ________________ while on a sea voyage you might get a visit from King Neptune.

c Each classroom opens onto the ________________.

d The ________________ had the orchestra practising for months for the concert.

e Mark Twain is the ________________ of the book *The Adventures of Tom Sawyer*.

f Snow White's stepmother spent hours admiring herself in the ________________.

g The teacher chose a ________________ to collect the lunch orders from the canteen.

h I have a real ________________ of snakes.

i Gavin plays in the ________________ football team, but his older brother plays with the seniors.

j The farmer bought a new ________________ just before harvesting.

Word Square

5 Can you arrange these eight words so that they all fit into the square?

meet	snap	pest	line
nine	slam	ante	ants

Does It Make Sense?

6 Put or into the gaps only if it makes a word.

auth ___ ___	tig ___ ___	sn ___ ___ e
horr ___ ___	sc ___ ___ e	leath ___ ___
golf ___ ___	anch ___ ___	man ___ ___
tut ___ ___	edit ___ ___	teach ___ ___
monit ___ ___	alligat ___ ___	sn ___ ___ kel
c ___ ___ e	qu ___ ___ ter	ord ___ ___
cl ___ ___	equat ___ ___	dr ___ ___ n
st ___ ___ e	str ___ ___	sw ___ ___ e
th ___ ___ n	az ___ ___ e	t ___ ___ ch

Glido Words

7 Use the clues to complete the puzzle.

a	r				
b		r			
c			r		
d				r	
e					r
f				r	
g			r		
h		r			
i	r				

a A firearm with a long barrel
b The main stem of a tree
c The earth including everything on it
d To frighten or to startle
e A large ship on a regular shipping line
f Something extra; not being used
g Cheerful and happy; joyful
h Daring or courageous
i Correct or true; opposite of wrong

Anagrams EA

8 **a** Change drier into a person on a horse. ____________

b Change tap into a word meaning appropriate. ____________

c Change dune into a word meaning without clothes. ____________

d Change groan into a musical instrument. ____________

e Change pier into ready to be picked and eaten. ____________

f Change livers into a precious metal. ____________

g Change canter into a sleep-like condition of the mind. ____________

h Change race into a word meaning to be concerned. ____________

i Change cork into popular modern music. ____________

j Change bore into a long flowing garment. ____________

Challenge words

Find the meaning of these or words and learn how to spell them.

elevator	manor	snorkel	radiator	councillor
alligator	error	aviator	transport	professor

ue words

continue	tissue	issue	rescue	due
pursue	argue	statue	avenue	value

1 **Write each of the list words in your book. Use four of the words in sentences of your own.**

2 **Circle the correct definition to go with the list word.**

a Due means
- drops of moisture which cover the ground early in the morning
- a person whose parents are Hebrew or Jewish
- a very small part or amount
- owing; not paid.

b An avenue is
- an enclosed space near a building
- a street shaped in a curve like the new moon
- a wide street usually with trees on both sides
- a rough path through forests or fields.

c Tissue is
- long strips of silvery sparkling material used to decorate Christmas trees
- the substance of which flesh and muscle is made
- a slight quarrel or disagreement
- a piece of baked clay.

d Issue means
- to give something out
- a crowd or mass of people
- to gasp for breath
- to sneeze quickly and make a sound.

3 **Write the list words in alphabetical order.**

______________ ______________ ______________ ______________ ______________

______________ ______________ ______________ ______________ ______________

Synonyms

Something to remember

Synonyms are words that have the same or similar meanings. For example:

slender—slim empty—vacant

4 **Choose words from the box below that are synonyms for the words in the columns. Write the words you choose on the lines.**

peculiar	answer	slay	gigantic	catastrophe	pester
friendly	pursue	toil	amaze	threaten	argue

enormous	________________	kill	________________
reply	________________	chase	________________
dispute	________________	odd	________________
amiable	________________	menace	________________
astonish	________________	work	________________
disaster	________________	annoy	________________

5 **Look at each word in the first column. Then, from the group of words opposite it, circle the word that is its synonym.**

student	eye, pupil, teacher
teacher	instructor, student, school
sly	cunning, annoying, laughing
own	owl, possess, sell
shy	loud, noisy, timid
stubborn	cunning, obstinate, friendly
total	less, sum, fire-ban
stop	go, advance, cease
squander	save, deposit, waste
grave	crave, serious, gravel

6 **Fill the gaps in these sentences with list words.**

a The plane is ________________ to land at four o'clock today.

b The children started to ________________ about whose turn it was to bat.

c The ________________ was lined with trees on both sides.

d The police officer started to __________________ the bankrobber on foot.

e When the fragile vase was posted it was wrapped in __________________ paper and placed in a strong cardboard box.

f The fireman went to the __________________ of the child trapped in the burning building.

g Mrs Teilhard will __________________ as Club President.

h The expert set a __________________ of $100 000 on the painting.

i In the city square was a __________________ of one of the pioneers of the district.

j Taxation was the main __________________ that people spoke about just before the election.

Word Square

7 **The answers to this word square are the same down as across. Use the clues to fill in the square.**

Clues: **1** A type of bag for moving goods

2 The measure of a surface

3 Hardens (like jelly when it cools down)

4 Not difficult

1			
2			
3			
4			

Front and Back

EA

8 **Each of these words begin and end with the same two letters. Use the clues to help you fill in the missing letter.**

___ ___ adac ___ ___ A pain in the skull

___ ___ ur ___ ___ A building for Christian worship

___ ___ rmina ___ ___ To bring to an end

___ ___ otogra ___ ___ A picture obtained with a camera

___ ___ ti ___ ___ To stop working because of age

___ ___ at ___ ___ A public speaker

___ ___ cap ___ ___ Reaches freedom; gets away

___ ___ i ___ ___ A round white vegetable

___ ___ sto ___ ___ To bring back to original state

___ ___ n ___ ___ Sight, hearing, taste, touch or smell

ough words

ought	bought	thought	fought	brought
nought	sought	tough	rough	cough

1 **Write each of the list words in your book. Use four of the words in sentences of your own.**

2 **Fill the gaps in these sentences with list words.**

a In the ancient Greek myth, Theseus ________________ the Minotaur in the labryinth.

b Jayne ________________ the mail in from the letterbox.

c The people next door to us ________________ a new caravan yesterday.

d Eight followed by a ________________ represents the number 80.

e He ________________ to look after the children.

f Yesterday I stood in the rain at the football match and today I have a very bad ________________.

g That tabletop is made of very ________________ plastic.

h It's not the gift, it's the ________________ that counts.

i We ________________ to change her mind, but she resisted our arguments.

j Some people say that football is a ________________ game.

3 **Write the list words in three groups according to how they sound.**

Group A ______________ ______________ ______________ ______________

______________ ______________ ______________

Group B ______________ ______________

Group C ______________

4 **Write the list words in alphabetical order.**

______________ ______________ ______________ ______________ ______________

______________ ______________ ______________ ______________ ______________

5 Match the list word to the definition.

Past tense of buy ______________

Hard to break or cut ______________

The process or action of thinking ______________

To force air from the lungs noisily and sharply ______________

A verb expressing duty ______________

Past tense of fight ______________

Past tense of bring ______________

Nothing ______________

Not smooth or level ______________

Past tense of seek ______________

Fits to a 't'

6 Use the clues to find these words. They all start with w and end in t.

a An Australian marsupial which burrows in the ground and has soft hair, short legs and a thick body

b A small flat leather case for papers and paper money

c Something needed on a pitch to play a cricket match

d Heaviness

e An edible nut which has a rough shell divided into two parts

a	w					t
b	w				t	
c	w					t
d	w					t
e	w					t

An 'm' Puzzle

7

a	m							
b	m							
c	m							
d	m							
e	m							
f	m							

a To combine to form a whole
b An ancient story, usually religious or magical, which explains natural or historical events
c Greater in size; also a middle-ranking officer in the army
d Movable, not fixed; also art hung up on wires or string so that it is moved by currents of air
e A yellow-flowered plant with seeds from which a hot-tasting powder can be made
f A performer, writer, or student of music

Add an 'a'

8 **Add an a to each of these words to form a new word. The a may be added anywhere in the word, but the other letters must remain in the same order, for example, lunch—launch.**

led	____________	mid	____________	men	____________	net	____________
or	____________	cot	____________	pint	____________	met	____________
manger	____________	nil	____________	pin	____________	place	____________
prise	____________	pry	____________	rid	____________		

Word Quiz EA

9 **How quickly can you find these words?**

a A seven-letter word ending in ley ____________
b A seven-letter word ending in the ____________
c A five-letter word ending in the ____________
d A six-letter word ending in lth ____________
e A seven-letter word ending in per ____________
f A four-letter word ending in ro ____________
g A five-letter word ending in io ____________
h A five-letter word ending in no ____________

ear words

nearly	tear	learn	year	earth
disappear	earn	search	heard	early

1 **Write each of the list words in your book. Use four of the words in sentences of your own.**

2 **Unjumble the list word in each sentence.**

a The (hrasec) for the missing aeroplane was called off after six days. ____________

b To our amazement we watched the genie (sadapiper) into a cloud of smoke. ____________

c My sister is ten years old and my brother is (ranyel) eight. ____________

d The lost boy had a (rate) in the corner of his eye. ____________

e Every morning Susie gets up (relay) and goes for a three kilometre run. ____________

f Next (raye) my sister is going to Japan as an exchange student. ____________

g David tried hard last night to (realn) the eight times table. ____________

h The (teahr) travels around the sun. ____________

i Ingrid said she could (rane) up to twenty dollars a week delivering pamphlets for the local supermarket. ____________

j Shannon (hdear) the sound of the jet, but she couldn't see it in the sky. ____________

Alphabetical Order

3 **Place the ear words in each group in alphabetical order.**

a	dear	tear	gear	year	appear
	____________	____________	____________	____________	____________
b	disappear	spear	near	shear	clear
	____________	____________	____________	____________	____________
c	earth	ear	fear	early	earn
	____________	____________	____________	____________	____________
d	learn	heard	search	rear	hear
	____________	____________	____________	____________	____________

Apostrophe of Possession

Something to remember

We have used apostrophes (') before when writing contractions such as we have = we've (see page 36). We also use apostrophes to show ownership. For example:

The dog's collar is very dirty.

Note:

a If the noun is singular we add 's to show ownership.

dog—The dog's collar is very dirty.

city—The city's tram system is very old.

b If the noun is plural and ends in s we just add an apostrophe at the end of the word.

cities—The cities' mayors met for lunch.

coaches—The coaches' forum discussed the new rules.

c If the noun is plural but does not end in s we add 's.

men—The men's tennis final will be played today.

children—The children's books are in the classroom.

4 Using the rules above, complete each sentence by writing the possessive form of the word in brackets.

- **a** Will got a job cleaning out the (horse) ________________ stable.
- **b** The (butterflies) ________________ wings were a mass of different colours in the sky.
- **c** On display on the front counter were the (men) ________________ socks.
- **d** The (lizard) ________________ tail dropped off when Jemma went to pick it up.
- **e** My cousin, Alex, goes to a (boy) ________________ school.
- **f** Dad made a new (dog) ________________ kennel for Buster.
- **g** At the party the (fairies) ________________ wands were all in a neat pile.
- **h** The (drover) ________________ dog rounded up the stray cattle.

5 Write the following using apostrophes of possession.

- **a** the hats of the soldiers ________________
- **b** the crown of the king ________________
- **c** the wing of the fly ________________
- **d** the wings of the flies ________________
- **e** the corners of the boxes ________________
- **f** the toys of the children ________________

T-sers

6 Unjumble the letters.

a Add t to heart and get a warning of harm or injury to a person. ____________

b Add t to ranges and get a word meaning unusual; not known or familiar. ____________

c Add t to soul and get a water lily that grows in some hot countries. ____________

d Add t to elf and get the side opposite to the right. ____________

e Add t to rings and get a thick thread or a cord used for tying up parcels. ____________

f Add t to chip and get the ground between the wickets in the game of cricket. ____________

g Add t to sap and get a word meaning having happened in earlier times. ____________

h Add t to chip and get the level of a musical note, whether high or low. (What do you notice about this answer?) ____________

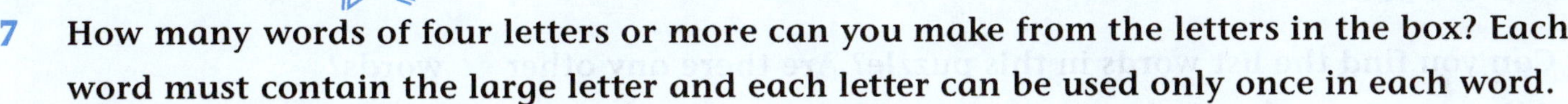

Word Puzzle

7 How many words of four letters or more can you make from the letters in the box? Each word must contain the large letter and each letter can be used only once in each word.

h	t	s
	c	o
u	e	r

____________ ____________ ____________ ____________

____________ ____________ ____________ ____________

____________ ____________ ____________ ____________

____________ ____________ ____________ ____________

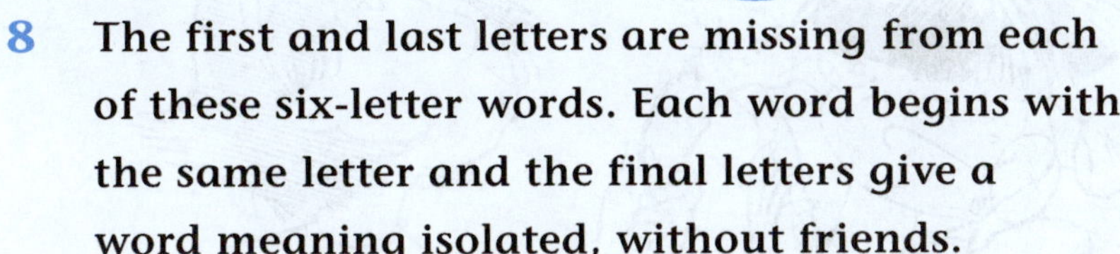

A Word by Itself

8 The first and last letters are missing from each of these six-letter words. Each word begins with the same letter and the final letters give a word meaning isolated, without friends.

	e	r	e	a	
	u	c	k	o	
	o	t	t	o	
	h	a	n	c	
	a	n	c	e	
	e	l	e	r	

ee words

screen	steel	freeze	bleed	squeeze
kneel	toffee	sneeze	degree	feeble

1 **Write each of the list words in your book. Use four of the words in sentences of your own.**

2 **Unjumble the list word in each sentence.**

a The fog acted as a (recsen) for the smugglers. ______________

b When you have a cold you often (neseez). ______________

c The soldier had to (neelk) before the queen when he was knighted. ______________

d The truck delivered a lot of (tesel) for the new building. ______________

e If you want to crack walnuts you can (uezqsee) them together. ______________

f The temperature has only dropped one (gereed) in the last hour. ______________

g When Jan cut her finger she started to (lebed) all over the floor. ______________

h The old woman is too (eeefbl) to do her own shopping. ______________

i It was so cold outside I thought my blood was going to (zeefer). ______________

j For our school festival I helped Dad make a tray of (feetof). ______________

Word Search

3 **Can you find the list words in this puzzle? Are there any other ee words? Colour in the ee words you find.**

y	e	l	e	e	f	s
o	s	c	r	e	e	n
s	t	o	f	f	e	e
q	e	g	r	d	b	e
u	e	l	e	e	l	z
e	l	e	e	g	e	e
e	s	e	z	r	j	a
z	k	n	e	e	l	n
e	s	b	l	e	e	d

4 **Arrange the following groups of ee words into alphabetical order.**

a	freeze	bleed	kneel	toffee	degree
	______	______	______	______	______
b	feeble	fleece	needle	steed	jamboree
	______	______	______	______	______
c	reindeer	indeed	freeway	referee	deepen
	______	______	______	______	______
d	steel	screen	squeeze	sneeze	steeple
	______	______	______	______	______
e	volunteer	cheese	eerie	beetle	speech
	______	______	______	______	______
f	exceed	beehive	proceed	queer	glee
	______	______	______	______	______

Word Steps

5 **Use the clues to find these ee words.**

a	_	_	e	e				
b	_	_	e	e	_			
c	_	_	e	e	_	_		
d	_	_	e	e	_	_	_	
e	_	_	e	e	_	_	_	_
f	_	_	e	e	_	_	_	
g	_	_	e	e	_	_		
h	_	_	e	e	_			
i	_	_	e	e				

a To run away (especially from danger)

b A very strong metal made from iron

c To make a sudden blowing noise through the nose

d A leopard-like animal

e Bright and lively; happy

f A plant, such as ivy, that grows along the ground or up a wall

g To become ice; to feel very cold

h To lose blood

i The joint in the middle part of the leg

Word Square

6

c	e	o	s
a	p	t	m
f	m	e	a
a	e	r	t

List as many words as you can from the letters in the word square. Each word must be made up of letters in squares which touch each other.

______________ ______________ ______________ ______________

______________ ______________ ______________ ______________

______________ ______________ ______________ ______________

______________ ______________ ______________ ______________

Does It Make Sense?

7 **Add ee into the gaps where it will make a word. Use a dictionary if you are not sure.**

squ ___ ___ ze	___ ___ ght	v ___ ___ l
toff ___ ___	degr ___ ___	sl ___ ___ gh
f ___ ___ ble	v ___ ___ n	coff ___ ___
___ ___ rie	fl ___ ___ ce	th ___ ___ f
b ___ ___ tle	v ___ ___ w	d ___ ___ pen
st ___ ___ ple	f ___ ___ ld	exc ___ ___ d

Fits to a 't' 

8 **Use the clues to find these words that all start with b and end in t.**

a	b					t
b	b					t
c	b					t
d	b					t
e	b					t
f	b					t
g	b					t
h	b					t

a A container made of woven sticks or similar material

b A dance in which a story is told without speech or singing

c Something long with a rounded end which is fired from a gun

d A round head-covering tied under the chin, usually worn by babies

e Giving out or throwing back light very strongly

f A paper used to vote

g A round, open metal or plastic container with a handle for carrying liquids

h A meal laid out for guests who serve themselves

Challenge words

Find the meaning of these ee words and learn how to spell them.

committee	creed	preen	spree	wheeze
corroboree	guarantee	proceed	succeed	exceed

oo words

rooster	shampoo	harpoon	bamboo	toothache
moose	cartoon	lagoon	igloo	cocoon

1 **Write each of the list words in your book. Use four of the words in sentences of your own.**

2 **Use the clues to complete each word.**

a A large deer with very large, flat horns that lives in North America ___ oo ___ ___

b A protective case of silky threads in which a pupa is enclosed ___ ___ ___ oo ___

c A sharp spear attached to a rope, used for hunting whales ___ ___ ___ ___ oo ___

d A lake of sea water partly or completely separated from the sea ___ ___ ___ oo ___

e An adult male chicken ___ oo ___ ___ ___

f A pain in your teeth ___ oo ___ ___ ___ ___ ___ ___

g A kind of very tall grass with stiff hollow stems which are used for making furniture ___ ___ ___ ___ oo

h A short, funny film or drawing in a newspaper ___ ___ ___ ___ oo ___

i A liquid soap-like product used to wash your hair ___ ___ ___ ___ ___ oo

j A hut made of blocks of hard snow with a domed roof ___ ___ ___ oo

Hidden Words

3 **Which six list words are hidden here? Each word is in two parts.**

toon	loo	bam
ache	sham	tooth
goon	la	ig
car	poo	boo

____

____

____

Verb Tenses

Something to remember

All sentences contain a verb, which is an action word. For example:

When he was younger my Dad played football for Essendon.

The tense of a verb tells us whether the action occurred in the past, the present or the future.

Past tense: I played netball for the Kestrals last year.

Present tense: I play netball for the Kestrals every weekend.

Future tense: I will play netball for the Kestrals next season.

4 Underline the verb in these sentences. Then say whether the verb is in the past, present or future tense.

- **a** Gillian was chosen as class captain. ____________
- **b** The wind blew the leaves all around the yard. ____________
- **c** The lizard is sleeping in the sun. ____________
- **d** Taree will play the piano at the concert. ____________
- **e** Because my bike had a flat tyre, I walked to my nanna's. ____________
- **f** Mr Jenkins taught me in Year 4. ____________
- **g** That vine is growing all over the fence. ____________
- **h** I'll send you an email tomorrow. ____________

5 Complete these statements by adding a verb in the past tense.

- **a** Today I laugh. Yesterday I ____________.
- **b** Today I sing. Yesterday I ____________.
- **c** Today I hear. Yesterday I ____________.
- **d** Today I cough. Yesterday I ____________.
- **e** Today I teach. Yesterday I ____________.
- **f** Today I sleep. Yesterday I ____________.
- **g** Today I fly. Yesterday I ____________.
- **h** Today I hide. Yesterday I ____________.

Word Chain

6 Change give to take in four moves by changing one letter at a time to form a new word.

g	i	v	e
t	a	k	e

7 **Fill the gaps in these sentences with list words.**

a Lara had to go to the dentist because she had a ____________ .

b To make the ____________ the Inuit first began to cut large blocks of snow.

c When I stay at my uncle's farm I can hear a ____________ crowing every morning.

d The Inuit carefully stood up in his canoe and threw his ____________ at the seal.

e The water in the ____________ was calm as it was sheltered from the wind.

f In some parts of the world a ____________ is called an elk.

g The caterpillar spun a ____________.

h My favourite ____________ in the newspaper is *Snake Tales*.

i While Gwenda was washing her hair she got ____________ in her eyes.

j Pandas eat ____________.

Find the Word

8 Letters 4, 5, 3, 2 are a type of tall plant with a trunk and branches.
Letters 5, 6, 1 mean to take another person's property unlawfully.
The whole word is a plant with a large, round red root, cooked and eaten as a vegetable.
(It's a oo word, too.)

1	2	3	4	5	6	7	8

Block Out

FUN

9 **Every time you see a list word, cross it out. You'll be left with a message giving you some interesting information.**

rooster	cartoon	giraffes	moose	are
very	shy	lagoon	timid	cartoon
bamboo	rooster	animals	that	lagoon
would	rather	moose	run	cocoon
away	toothache	igloo	harpoon	than
shampoo	lagoon	fight	igloo	they
can	cocoon	run	very	harpoon
moose	fast	with	a	bamboo
top	speed	harpoon	around	forty-five
kilometres	shampoo	per	igloo	hour

Easily confused words

accept	quiet	practice	stationery	desert
except	quite	practise	stationary	dessert

1 **Write each of the list words in your book.**

2 **Look at the meanings of each pair of words, and then write the words in the correct sentences.**

Accept means to receive something or to agree with something.

Except means excluding or leaving something or someone out.

a We are all going to the show ____________ Kim.

b Michael Clarke went on stage to ____________ the award.

Quiet means without noise, while quite means completely or totally.

a The runner fell to the ground ____________ exhausted.

b It was so ____________ in the room you could hear the wall clock ticking.

Practice is a noun meaning a habit or custom.

Practise is a verb, something you do regularly.

a I will ____________ the piano every night this week.

b I'll be going to netball ____________ after school.

Stationery means all types of writing materials, while stationary means standing still.

a The car with the flat battery was ____________ .

b Before school started Mum bought all my ____________ from the local newsagent.

A desert is a dry region that is usually sandy.

Desserts are the sweets we have at the end of a meal.

a For ____________ we had fruit salad and ice cream.

b Camels are used a lot for travelling in the ____________ .

3 **Write the list words in alphabetical order.**

____________ ____________ ____________ ____________ ____________

____________ ____________ ____________ ____________ ____________

4 **Use the clues to find these words that start and end with t.**

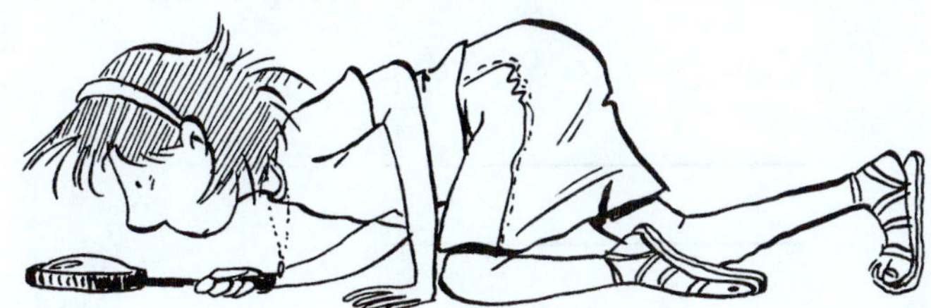

a	t					t
b	t					t
c	t					t
d	t					t
e	t					t
f	t					t
g	t					t
h	t					t

a A small round block of medicine
b Past tense of the verb teach
c A person with complete power who rules cruelly and unjustly
d To push forcefully and suddenly
e A printed piece of paper allowing you to journey on a bus or enter a theatre
f A special ability or skill especially of a high quality
g Anything at which shots or missiles are aimed
h A sensation of dryness in the mouth caused by the need to drink

5 **Use the clues and see if you can find these ic words. The first one has been done for you.**

a The ic that is a severe stomach ache. colic
b The ic that is related to the whole universe. ___ ___ ___ ___ ic
c The ic that is exciting, relating to drama. ___ ___ ___ ___ ___ ___ ic
d The ic that causes pity or sorrow. ___ ___ ___ ___ ___ ___ ic
e The ic that is the adding, subtracting, etc. of numbers. ___ ___ ___ ___ ___ ___ ___ ___ ic
f The ic that is a measurement system based on the metre. ___ ___ ___ ___ ic
g The ic that is to do with the sense of sight. ___ ___ ___ ic
h The ic that means to play and jump about gaily. ___ ___ ___ ___ ic
i The ic that means making a good photograph. ___ ___ ___ ___ ___ ___ ___ ___ ___ ___ ic
j The ic that means having the talent to write poetry. ___ ___ ___ ___ ic

Compound Words

6 Match a word from List A with a word from List B to make a compound word.

List A	List B	Compound Words
else	writer	________________
ear	saver	________________
type	light	________________
sun	where	________________
thunder	bread	________________
life	lid	________________
ginger	flower	________________
candle	storm	________________
grass	ache	________________
eye	hopper	________________

Use three of the compound words in sentences of your own.

a ____

b ____

c ____

History of Words 

7 Match these words with their historical clues.

asparagus bonfire tremendous alphabet automobile

a This word once meant something that made people tremble, for example, a fire that was out of control or a plague. Today it would apply to something that is great or outstanding. ______________

b This word originally meant 'a fire of bones' and was once the method used to dispose of the carcasses of animals and humans. ______________

c This word comes from the Greek word *autos*, meaning self, and the Latin word *mobilis*, meaning movable, so it is a self-movable machine. ______________

d In the eighteenth century people called this 'sparrow grass', but the word actually comes from an old Latin word meaning 'sprout' or 'shoot'. ______________

e This word comes from ancient Greece. It is made up of the first two Greek letters, alpha and beta. Greek children would say 'alpha, beta, gamma, delta,' the same way that we would say 'a, b, c, d'. ______________

Revision

1 Choose the correct word.

pracktise	praktice	practise	______________
pickture	picture	pictor	______________
mirror	miror	mirrer	______________
persue	purshoo	pursue	______________
coff	cough	kough	______________
nort	nought	gnawrt	______________
tempreture	temperture	temperature	______________
quiet	kwiet	quyet	______________
deckorate	decorate	decerate	______________
kneel	neel	kneal	______________
toffee	tofee	toffe	______________
coocon	cocoon	cercoon	______________
hearrd	heard	hurd	______________
ruff	wruff	rough	______________
disappear	dissapear	disapear	______________
toothake	toothacke	toothache	______________

2 Write these words into your book and group them into word families.

nature	author	brought	value	earth
freeze	rooster	bamboo	kneel	year
pleasure	tractor	issue	nought	toffee
squeeze	equator	moose	cartoon	measure
rescue	disappear	decorate	rough	

3 Find small words that are in the larger words.

capture	______________	furniture	______________	corridor	______________
continue	______________	thought	______________	issue	______________
lagoon	______________	practise	______________	toffee	______________
cartoon	______________	figure	______________	harpoon	______________
literature	______________	toothache	______________	monitor	______________
conductor	______________	quite	______________	nearly	______________
disappear	______________	learn	______________	search	______________

4 Look at these words. Use them to answer each question.

iron	year	earth	climb	rooster
cough	disappear	toffee	avenue	tractor
mirror	manufacture			

a Which words begins with a prefix meaning *not*? ______________

b Which word ends in a silent letter? ______________

c Which word might you use when playing golf? ______________

d Which word has four syllables? ______________

e Which word could become very sticky? ______________

f Which word is a type of bird? ______________

g Which word always looks back at you? ______________

h Which word is a period of time? ______________

i Which word is something you could get in winter? ______________

j Which word is a type of street? ______________

k Which word is very useful on a farm? ______________

l Which word is dirty? ______________

Jumbled Words

5 Unjumble each word. Then write the plural for each word. The first one has been done for you.

rimorr	mirror	mirrors
cipuret	______________	______________
situes	______________	______________
eestdsr	______________	______________
acttrro	______________	______________
veuane	______________	______________
reedeg	______________	______________
sootrer	______________	______________
snilad	______________	______________
rate	______________	______________
someo	______________	______________
nagit	______________	______________
cesern	______________	______________

A Giant Crossword

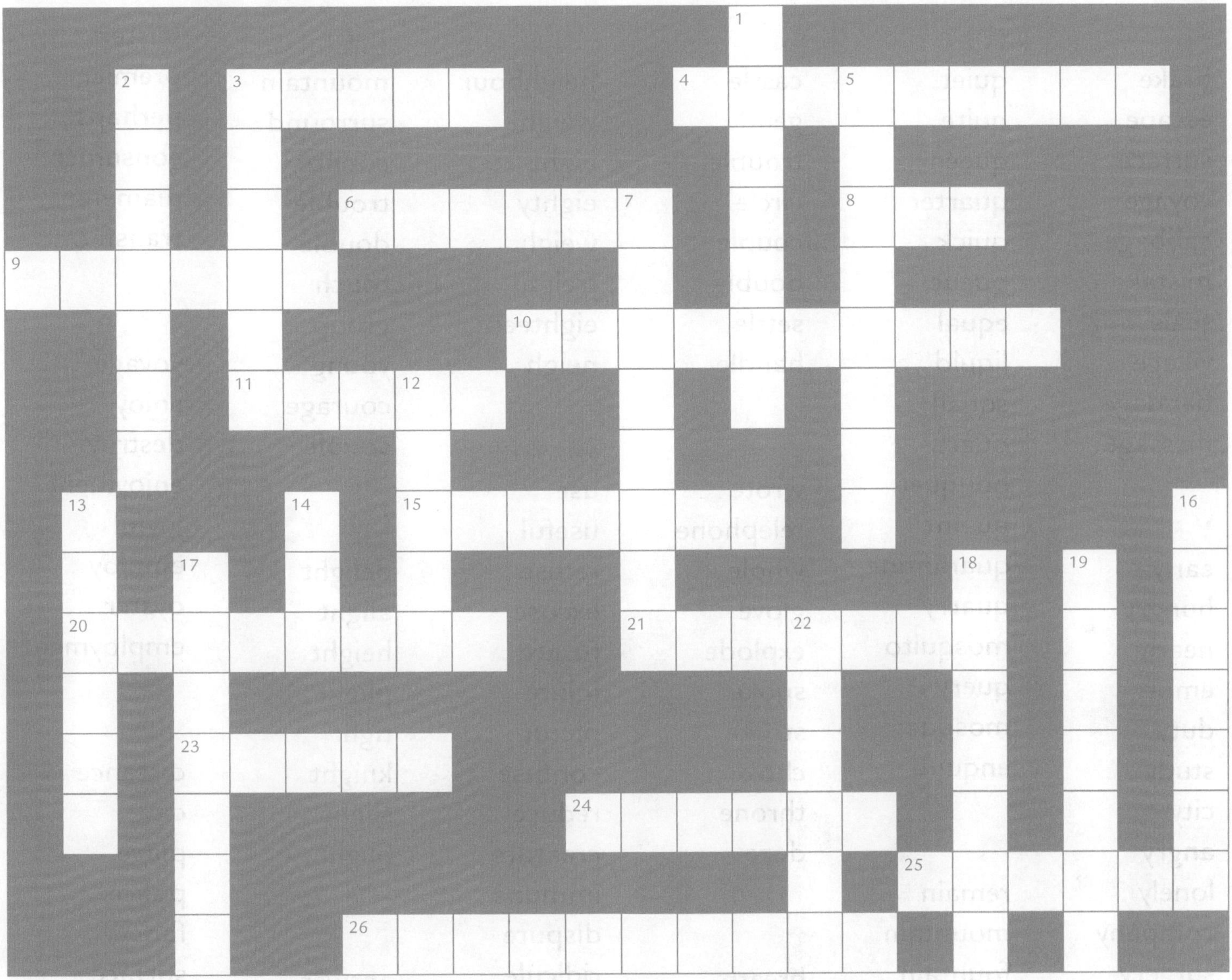

Across:

3 Daring or courageous
4 To bring to an end
6 Past tense of buy
8 Cunning
9 Weak
10 Teacher
11 Poisonous
15 Unusual; not known or familiar
20 Waste
21 An old word for the pilot of an aircraft
23 Funny magazine
24 Zero
25 Antonym for conceal
26 Standing still

Down:

1 To bring back to original state
2 Antonym for captivity
3 A paper used to vote
5 A performer, writer or student of music
7 Island state of Australia
12 To give something out
13 Synonym for annoy
14 A person's closest relatives
16 An air tube that sits above the surface of the water allowing a swimmer below to breath
17 To do well, to achieve a purpose
18 A plant such as ivy which grows along the ground or up a wall
19 An adult male chicken
22 The writer of a book, play or article

List and Challenge words

a–e
brake
escape
surface
voyage
cabbage
mistake
scale
village
bandage
message

y = 'e'
early
hungry
nearly
empty
duty
study
city
angry
lonely
company
surgery
cemetery
authority
majority
annually
oddity
machinery
equally
ability
finally

qu
quiet
quite
queen
quarter
quick
queue
equal
liquid
squall
quartz
bouquet
quaint
quarantine
quarry
mosquito
query
mosque
enquire

ai
remain
mountain
fountain
tailor
against
explain
curtain
certain
frail
strain

le
castle
gentle
trouble
circle
couple
double
settle
handle

o–e
wrote
telephone
whole
glove
explode
spoke
stroke
choke
throne
doze

ea
breath
meant
wealth
health
breakfast
instead
steady
death
weather
already

eigh
neighbour
weight
eight
eighty
weigh
freight
eighteen
neigh

u–e
use
useful
refuse
excuse
future
injure
picture
confuse
reduce
creature
immune
dispute
ridicule
exclude
tribute
acute
conclude
globule
presume
volume

ou
mountain
surround
country
trouble
double
touch
group
young
courage
couple

igh
delight
alight
height
plight
tight
knight
slight
blight

er
answer
several
herd
proper
general
either
butcher
modern
neither
desert
flounder
whether
retriever
lantern
blister
premier
perhaps
consumer
diameter
transfer

oy
voyage
enjoy
destroy
enjoyment
joyful
employ
oyster
employment

soft c
distance
city
place
police
fancy
surface
sentence
circle
office
ceiling

au
cause
aunt
taught
daughter
auction
because
caught
naughty
slaughter
autumn
applause
exhaust
pauper
authentic
fraud
daub
nausea
tarpaulin
audition
cauliflower

oar
oar
roar
hoard
cupboard
coarse
soar
boar
board
cardboard
hoarse

tch
latch
stretch
batch
stretcher
clutch
stitch
fetch
pitch
dispatch
hutch

soft g
engine
garage
orange
savage
agent
engineer
judge
gentle
sponge
tragic
average
suggest
generation
enrage
lounge
gymnasium
revenge
general
oblige
genuine

se
sense
else
lose
choose
rouse
surprise
please
loose
tease
excuse

are
scare
stare
beware
bare
spare
parents
hardware
prepare
compare
declare

or
mirror
horror
decorate
corridor
tractor
author
conductor
junior
monitor
equator
elevator
manor
snorkel
radiator
councillor
alligator
error
aviator
transport
professor

ee
screen
steel
freeze
bleed
squeeze
kneel
toffee
sneeze
degree
feeble
committee
creed
preen
spree
wheeze
corroboree
guarantee
proceed
succeed
exceed

ph
graph
telephone
nephew
orphan
telegraph
elephant
photograph
autograph
alphabet
atmosphere
pheasant
philosopher
phlegm
pharmacy
physical
physician
phrase
phlox
phantom
epitaph

ue
continue
tissue
issue
rescue
due
pursue
argue
statue
avenue
value

oo
rooster
shampoo
harpoon
bamboo
toothache
moose
cartoon
lagoon
igloo
cocoon

ure
nature
picture
capture
measure
figure
furniture
pleasure
temperature
literature
manufacture

ough
ought
bought
thought
fought
brought
nought
sought
tough
rough
cough

ear
nearly
tear
learn
year
earth
disappear
earn
search
heard
early

Australian history

discovery
colony
Aborigine
explore
rebellion
convict
governor
settlement
marine
grazier

The Great Barrier Reef

coral
shellfish
tourists
marine
sanctuary
submerged
biologists
Queensland
crustaceans
cays
barrier
fauna
wildlife
sea-urchins
flora
species
crayfish
herons
anemone
gannets
marlin
invertebrates
beche-de-mer
gulf
terns
Gladstone

Easily confused words

accept
quiet
practice
stationery
desert
except
quite
practise
stationary
dessert

Commonly misspelt words

separate
accommodation
embarrass
signature
straight
queue
necessary
argument
thought
cupboard

agent
agency

alight
alighted

allow
allowable
allowably
allowance
allowed
allowing

alphabet
alphabetical
alphabetically

angry
angrier
angriest
angrily

answer
answerable
answered
answerer
answering

argue
arguable
arguably
argued
arguing
argument
argumentative

atmosphere
atmospheric

bandage
bandaged
bandaging

batch
batched
batches

bleed
bled
bleeder
bleeding

brake
braked
braking

breath
breathalysed
breathalyser
breathe
breathed
breather
breathing
breathless
breathtaking

capture
captor
captured
capturer
capturing

cartoon
cartooned
cartoonish
cartoonist

cause
causal
causation
causative
caused
causing

certain
certainly
certainty
certainties
certitude

choke
choked
choker
choking

circle
circled
circling
circular

city
cities

coarse
coarser
coarsest
coarsely
coarsen
coarsened
coarseness
coarsening

cocoon
cocooned
cocooning

collar
collared
collarbone
collaring

company
companies

compare
comparable
comparably
comparative
comparatively
compared
comparing
comparison

confuse
confused
confusing
confusion

continue
continual
continually
continuance
continuation
continued
continuing
continuity
continuous

cough
coughed
coughing

country
countries
countrified
countrify
countryman
countrywoman
countrymen
countrywomen

courage
courageous

crease
creased
creasing

curtain
curtain-up
curtain-raiser

declare
declaration
declaratory
declared
declaring

decorate
decorated
decorating
decoration
decorative
decorator

delight
delighted
delightful
delightfully
delighting

deliver
deliverance
delivered
deliverer
deliveries
delivering
delivery

desert
deserted
deserter
deserting
desertion

destroy
destroyed
destroyer
destroying
destructibility
destructible
destruction
destructive
destructor

direct
directed
directing
direction
directional
directive
director
directorate
directory
directories

disappear
disappearance
disappeared
disappearing

discover
discovered
discoverer
discovery
discoveries
discovering

disease
diseased

dispatch
dispatched
dispatcher
dispatching

distance
distant
distantly

doze
dozed
dozy
dozily
doziness
dozing

drill
drilled
drilling

due
duly

duty
duties
dutiful
dutifully
duty-free

dwell
dwelt
dwelled
dweller
dwelling

early
earlier
earliest
earliness

earn
earned
earner
earning

eight
eighteen
eighteenth
eighth
eightieth
eighty

elephant
elephantine

else
elsewhere

employ
employability
employable
employed
employee
employer
employing

empty
emptied
emptier
empties
emptiest
emptiness
emptying

engine
engineer
engineered
engineering

enjoy
enjoyable
enjoyably
enjoyed
enjoying
enjoyment

equal
equality
equalities
equalled
equalling
equally

equator
equatorial

escape
escaped
escapee
escaping
escapism
escapologist

excuse
excusable
excusably
excused

expert
expertise
expertly

explain
explainable
explained
explaining
explanation
explanatory

explode
exploded
exploding
explosion
explosive

fancy
fancied
fancier
fancies
fanciest
fanciful
fancifully
fancying

fetch
fetched
fetching

figure
figured
figurehead
figureless

final
finale
finalise
finalised
finalising
finalist
finality
finalities
finally

frail
frailer
frailest
frailty
frailties

freeze
freezer
freezing
froze
frozen

freight
freightage
freighter

further
furtherance
furthered
furthering
furthermore
furthermost
furthest

future
futurism
futurist
futuristic

garage
garaged

general
generality
generalities
generally

gentle
gentleness
gentler
gentlest

graph
graphic
graphical
graphically

group
grouped
grouping

handkerchief
handkerchiefs

handle
handlebar
handled
handler
handling

harpoon
harpooned
harpooner
harpooning

herd
herded
herdsman

hoard
hoarded
hoarder
hoarding

hoarse
hoarsely
hoarseness
hoarsest

hungry
hungrier
hungriest
hungrily

increase
increased
increasing

injure
injured
injuries
injuring
injurious
injury

iron
ironed
ironclad
ironmaster

island
islander
isle
islet

issue
issuance
issued
issuing

joyful
joy
joyfully
joyless
joyous
joyously
joyride
joyriding

judge
judged
judgement
judging

latch
latched
latches
latchkey

learn
learned
learner
learning
learnable
learnt

leash
leashes

liquid
liquidate
liquidated
liquidating
liquidation
liquidator
liquidity

lonely
lone
lonelier
loneliest
loneliness
loner
lonesome

lose
loser
losing
lost

manufacture
manufacturable
manufactured
manufacturer
manufacturing

measure
measurable
measured
measureless
measurement
measuring

million
millionaire
millionth

mirror
mirrored
mirroring

mistake
mistakable
mistaken
mistaking
mistook

modern
modernisation
modernise
modernised
modernising
modernism
modernity

monitor
monitored
monitoring

mountain
mountaineer
mountainous

naughty
naughtier
naughtiest
naughtily
naughtiness

neigh
neighed
neighing

neighbour
neighbourhood
neighbouring
neighbourliness
neighbourly

office
officer
official
officially

orphan
orphanage
orphaned

parents
parent
parentage
parental
parentally

photograph
photographed
photographer
photographic
photographing
photography

picture
pictured
picturesque
picturesqueness
picturing

pitch
pitchblende
pitched
pitches
pitcher
pitching

pleasure
pleasurable
pleasurably

plight
plighted

police
policed
policing

prepare
preparation
preparative
preparatory
prepared
preparedness
preparing

pursue
pursuance
pursuant
pursued
pursuer
pursuing
pursuit

quarter
quartered
quartering
quarterly
quartermaster

queue
queued
queues
queuing

quick
quicker
quickest
quickness
quicken

quiet
quieten
quietened
quietening
quieter
quietest
quietude
quietus

reason
reasonable
reasonably
reasoned

reduce
reduced
reducible
reducing
reduction

refuse
refusal
refused
refusing

remain
remainder
remained
remaining

rescue
rescued
rescuer
rescuing

roar
roared
roaring

rough
roughage
roughed
roughen
roughened
roughening
rougher
roughest
roughing
roughly
roughness

savage
savagedom
savagely
savagery

scale
scaled
scaling
scaly

scare
scarecrow
scared
scaring
scary

search
searched
searcher
searches
searching

season
seasonable
seasonably
seasonal
seasonally
seasoned
seasoning

sense
sensed
senseless
sensing
sensor

shampoo
shampooed
shampooing

slight
slighted
slighter
slightest

sneeze
sneezed
sneezing

soar
soared
soaring

spare
spared
sparing

sponge
sponged
sponger
sponging
spongy

squeeze
squeezed
squeezing

stare
stared
staring

statue
statuary
statuesque
statuette

steady
steadied
steadier
steadiest
steadily
steadiness
steadying

steel
steeled
steeling
steely

stitch
stitched
stitches
stitching

strain
strained
straining

stretch
stretched
stretcher
stretching

stroke
stroked
stroking

study
studied
studies
studious
studying

surface
surfaced
surfacing

surprise
surprised
surprising

surround
surrounded
surrounding

swallow
swallowed
swallowing
swallowtail

tailor
tailored
tailoring
tailor-made

tear
tearful
tearfully
tearless

tear
tearing
torn
tore

tease
teased
teaser
teasing

telephone
telephoned
telephonic
telephoning
telephonist
telephony

thought
thoughtful
thoughtfully
thoughtfulness
thoughtless

tight
tighten
tightened
tightening
tighter
tightest
tightly
tightrope
tights

touch
touched
touches
touchier
touchiest
touchiness
touching
touchy

tough
toughen
toughened
toughening
tougher
toughest
toughly

tragic
tragically

trouble
troubled
troublesome
troubling

use
usable
usage
used
useful
usefully
usefulness
useless
user
using

valley
valleys

value
valuable
valuation
valued
valueless
valuer
valuing

village
villager

voyage
voyaged
voyager
voyaging

warmth
warm
warmed
warmer
warmest

weigh
weighed
weighing

weight
weightily
weighting
weightless
weightlessness
weighty

whisper
whispered
whisperer
whispering

young
younger
youngest
youngster

Progress record sheet

Unit		Date completed	Comments: teacher, parents or student
Unit 1	**a–e** words		
Unit 2	**ea** words		
Unit 3	**o–e** words		
Unit 4	**u–e** words		
Unit 5	**y = ‘e’** words		
Unit 6	**ai** words		
Unit 7	**qu** words		
Unit 8	Australian history		
Unit 9	Revision		
Unit 10	**ou** words		
Unit 11	**er** words		
Unit 12	**soft c** words		
Unit 13	**le** words		
Unit 14	**oar** words		
Unit 15	**soft g** words		
Unit 16	**au** words		
Unit 17	Commonly misspelt words		
Unit 18	Revision		
Unit 19	**are** words		
Unit 20	**tch** words		
Unit 21	**se** words		
Unit 22	**ph** words		
Unit 23	**eigh** words		
Unit 24	**igh** words		
Unit 25	**oy** words		
Unit 26	The Great Barrier Reef		
Unit 27	Revision		
Unit 28	**ure** words		
Unit 29	**or** words		
Unit 30	**ue** words		
Unit 31	**ough** words		
Unit 32	**ear** words		
Unit 33	**ee** words		
Unit 34	**oo** words		
Unit 35	Easily confused words		
Unit 36	Revision		